GROWING UP
BY THE BOOK

DR PATRICIA WEERAKOON

Sexologist, therapist, best-selling author of
Teen Sex By the Book and *The Best Sex for Life*

An imprint of
Anglican Youthworks
PO Box A287
Sydney South NSW 1235
Australia

Ph: +61 2 8268 3344
Fax: +61 2 8268 3357
Email: sales@cepstore.com.au
Web: cepstore.com.au

Published October 2014.
Copyright © Patricia Weerakoon 2014.

This book is copyright. Apart from fair dealing for the purposes of private study, research, criticism and review as permitted under the Copyright Act, no part of this book may be reproduced by any process without the express permission of the publisher.

Scripture taken from The Holy Bible, NEW INTERNATIONAL VERSION®. Copyright © 1973, 1978, 1984, 2011 by Biblica, Inc. All rights reserved worldwide. Used by permission. NEW INTERNATIONAL VERSION® and NIV® are registered trademarks of Biblica, Inc. Use of either trademark for the offering of goods or services requires the prior written consent of Biblica US, Inc.

National Library of Australia
ISBN 978-1-925041-43-9

Managing editor—Julie Firmstone
Theological editors—Belinda Pollard, Marshall Ballantine-Jones
Illustrations—Lisa Flanagan
Cover design—Bethany Abbottsmith

Acknowledgement

To my son, Kamal,
who taught me everything I know about bringing up children.

Contents

A word to parents and carers	viii
Introduction	xi

Part 1 — 1

Chapter 1 | God's word on sex	2
Does God have a plan for sex?	6
Sex and relationships: why marriage is important	14
Chapter 2 | Your body: different and special	20
A body that's special to God	24
A body that's changing	25
Chapter 3 | Your brain: a work in progress	50
Getting to know your brain	50
Chapter 4 | Knowing who and whose you are	59
Who the world wants you to be	59
Being better or having more than others	60
Who Jesus says you are	67

Conclusion	75
Where have we been?	75
Where are we now?	76
Where are we going?	78

Part 2   79

Introduction	80
A–Z of topics	82
Abstinence	82
Anal sex	84
Aphrodisiac	85
Body image	86
Brazilian wax and other pubic hair removal	86
Bullying	87
Celibacy	89
Circumcision	89
Contraception	91
Chromosomes	92
Cyber bullying	93
Cyber communication	93
Dating	96
Depression	100
Erections and ejaculations	102
Homosexuality	104
Hymen	107
Intersex	107
Intimacy	108
Love	109

Masturbation	111
Menarche (menstrual period)	113
Modesty	117
Oral sex	119
Pornography (Porn)	120
Pubic area	125
Self-harm	125
Sexting	126
Sexual intercourse	127
Sexually transmitted infections (diseases)	128
Transgender	129
Virginity	130
Wet dreams	132

A word to parents and carers

Do you remember when you started puberty? Growing breasts and menstrual periods? Hair in strange places, acne and wet dreams? All of those hormones raging in your brain and body? I don't think any of us would want to go back. Would you?

So why do you need to share this book with your 10–14 year-old son or daughter? Haven't they had 'the sex talk' at school? Aren't they too young to know more than the basics of sex? After all, you're not qualified to talk to them about sex! You didn't get any sex education from your parents when you were young, and you turned out OK (well, sort of!).

Well thankfully, as a sexologist and researcher of more than 25 years' experience, I *am* qualified to talk with your child, and to encourage them to also talk with you.

So, let's get some facts straight right from the start.

1 | *You, parents, are your children's primary sex educators.* Even if you never have the formal 'sex talk' with them, everything that you do and

say—the way you respond to their questions and their behaviour—will influence their values and attitudes towards sexuality. Sex is 'caught and taught' in the family. The Bible is clear about your parental role in educating your children (Deuteronomy 11:18–20; Ephesians 6:4).

2 | *Sex education is more than 'just sex'.* It's about character. It's about teaching personal integrity and relational faithfulness within God's pattern for life. It's not about telling your children 'just don't do it'; it's about explaining God's plan to them (Proverbs 22:6), showing them why it's the best way to live, and demonstrating this in your own life.

3 | *As parents, be aware of what is happening in your child's life.* Today's children are 'digital natives': they're always connected via technology (even if you're controlling it), and they're totally comfortable and confident within the cyberworld. They're the most cyber-linked, advertised-to, and sexed-up generation ever. We need to help them navigate this exciting but scary new world, so they can make the most of the opportunities and avoid the dangers.

4 | *In addition to all this, kids today grow up faster.* Biologically, their hormones kick in at a younger age and they enter puberty earlier than you did. This means they are sexual at an earlier age and vulnerable to the pressures of a sexualised culture at a much younger age than you were.

5 | *Sometimes, in spite of all you do, things go wrong.* Your children are in a world where risk-taking is normal. Remember: God can forgive, heal and redeem anything. So can you. Be open, approachable, and available. Be the one they turn to when they need help, rather than friends and the internet.

This book doesn't just talk *at* your kids; it has activities designed to get them thinking and asking about sex and relationships, and about how they view themselves—their self-image.

# Ask Mum & Dad

Ask Mum and Dad sections encourage them to start a conversation with you about the topic they have just read, whether that's something sexual or the way they feel about their body or identity. Make the most of these opportunities. Don't be embarrassed—talk openly and honestly. The more comfortable you are, the more comfortable they'll be.

# Think spot

Think spots get the kids to reflect on something they've just learned. Ask your kids to share their thoughts with you if they feel comfortable about doing so.

# Alert

Alerts warn the children about unhealthy or dangerous ways of thinking and acting. Talk over these dangers with them.

Go ahead—be proactive. Be the parent God meant you to be. Guide and shape your child's knowledge, values and attitudes—before the world does.

Introduction

Today, sex is everywhere. Advertisers use it to sell everything from clothes and cars to magazines and music. There's heaps of stuff about sex on the internet and TV, and in books, movies and magazines. Your friends may even talk about sex. And you've probably been taught about sex in school.

We need to know about sex. Why? Because at some stage in our lives, all people have sexual feelings—even if they don't act on them. We all have some sense of what it means to 'be' sexual—even if we don't actually get involved in any sexual activity. Sex, romance and love are all really important. They deeply affect our sense of 'self'—'who' and 'what' we are.

This book looks at what it means to be a sexual person, but in the most important way: God's way. God's way is not about obeying rules; it doesn't just say 'do this' or 'don't do that'. Instead, it starts at the beginning. And the beginning is not us, but the God who created us and loves us.

This book explains how and why God made you the way he did: your sexual body, brain and feelings. Once we understand why God made us this way, we can live in harmony with his plans. And that's the way to have the happiest and healthiest life—including our sex life.

Why should you read this book?

If you're reading this book, you're likely to be aged somewhere between ten and 14 years, and someone (Mum, Dad, an aunty, uncle or youth leader) has given it to you. Why should you read it? Why do you need to learn about sex and relationships anyway? Maybe you've already been to the father–son or mother–daughter night at school. Or you think you have a pretty good idea about sex from magazines, the internet, video games, TV, music videos, and of course your friends.

You may know all you *want to know* at this point. 'I mean, oh my goodness! Getting the book was bad enough, but then Mum and Dad want to talk to me once I've finished it! How embarrassing!' Why would you talk to your parents about sex, relationships and how you feel about your body? What would they know about anything you're going through?

Your feelings are normal. You're not a child anymore; you don't look like a child anymore. Your body is changing. If you're a girl, you're developing breasts, curves and pubic hair, and you might have started menstruating. If you're a boy, you're getting body hair, your voice is changing and you're getting erections.

And, you don't feel like a child. Well, not all the time anyway; there are times when you want to climb into your parent's lap for a cuddle. At other times you don't want them anywhere near you; you want to do things your own way and explore your own identity.

These feelings are only some of the changes that will take place in your body and brain in the next few years. We'll talk more about these later in this book.

See? Maybe reading this book won't be so bad after all!

So, how do you manage all these changes? How do you decide 'your way'? Who (or where) do you go to for advice? The internet? TV? Magazines? Your favourite pop idol? Your friends? The cool kids at school?

God made you. He knew you before Mum's egg and Dad's sperm came together. The Bible says: 'For you created my inmost being; you knit me together in my mother's womb' (Psalm 139:13). God gives us his plan for living a good, happy and healthy life—and that includes your sex life. All you have to do is trust and follow him.

As you can see from my name on the cover, I am a doctor, and I have studied, researched and written about sex and relationships for a very long time! My job has been to talk about sex with young people like you, and older people like your parents. In doing so I've found that, whatever age you are, living your life according to God's plan is the best way! That's why I wrote this book for you.

In Part 1, we talk about how your body and brain are changing, and how this affects the way you feel about yourself and how you relate to others. We do all this in light of how God has made you, and his pattern for your life.

In Part 2, you'll find an A–Z of common sex terms. You may have heard of some or all of them. This section will give you the facts about these terms (and not what someone at school told you they mean!) so go to this section whenever you need to.

This book has activities for you to do, too—stuff for you to think through. There are also some suggested questions you can ask your parent(s) that will make talking about these things easier (and less embarrassing). As hard as it might be for you to imagine, they were once your age!

Think spot

Think spots are for you to stop and think about what you believe, how you feel, and what your friends talk about.

Alert

Alerts warn you about healthy or dangerous ways of thinking and acting. This information will prepare you to make wise and godly decisions.

Ask Mum & Dad

Ask Mum and Dad activities are opportunities for you to go and talk with your parents about sex, what growing up was like for them, and how they coped with the changes. It'll probably feel kind of weird at first. But remember: they want you to read this book! They know the book has these activities. And they're waiting to give you any help they can.

If you're ever confused, remember: you're not alone. Your parents, other family members, teachers, and church youth workers are all available to talk with you. So let them help you!

Once you've read this book, and talked with your parents, we hope you'll be able to understand and be comfortable with what it means to be a sexual person—God's way. We want you to live in the world as a happy, healthy, confident child of God, and avoid making the mistakes many other young people will make.

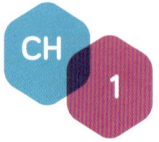

God's word on sex

Have you ever wondered whether God has anything to say about sex? What would your friends say if you asked them this question? Your parents—what would they say? And what is sex anyway?

 **Think spot**

What is sex?

You will come across Think spots as you read through this book. The idea is for you to spend a few minutes thinking about the topic that we'll be talking about. You may be surprised at how much you already know! Or you may find that some things that you have heard about or thought were right are actually lies.

Some of you may not want to write down your thoughts. You are not a writer. That's OK. However, I suggest that you create a document on your computer (iPad, phone, whatever) and make notes. Or you could get yourself a notebook to jot down your thoughts, and keep it somewhere safe. Save it: you may want to come back to it later and see if you think any differently after reading this book!

Here are the first questions:

1 | What comes into your mind when you think of the word 'sex'?

2 | What do you think your friends would say if you asked them?

3 | What about magazines, TV and the internet? What do they say about sex?

4 | Have you learned anything about sex at school?

What did you find?

You probably realise that sex can mean many things, depending on what you're doing and who you are with. Here are the three most important ways the word 'sex' is used.

1 | If you're filling in a form and they ask for your 'sex', they want to know whether you are a girl or a boy (female/male).

2 | At other times—for instance, when you are in a biology or PDHPE class—'sex' will be used to refer to the sexual parts of your body (the parts called the genitals: uterus, ovary, vagina, and vulva in girls and testes, scrotum, and penis in boys). The word is also used to describe the body changes of puberty (breasts, body hair and genital growth called secondary sexual characteristics).

The word 'sex' is also used to describe any and all forms of activity that are sexual. It is then called 'having sex' or 'sexual activity'. This can be something a person does alone, such as thinking about sex (called fantasy), or touching parts of their body to give themselves good sexual feelings (called masturbation or self-stimulation). More often 'having sex' is used to mean some form of sexual activity between two people. This covers a whole lot of activities: from kissing, cuddling and touching, through to a man and woman bringing their genital organs (penis and vagina) together in **SEXUAL INTERCOURSE**. Any sexual activity is special because it is the closest two people can ever get. Sexual intercourse (sometimes called coitus) is the end point of sexual activity. It is part of what the Bible refers to as 'one flesh' (Genesis 2:24). The intimacy of the man's penis in the woman's vagina and the sexual excitement that goes with it binds them together at body, brain and soul levels. In the Bible this is called a 'naked' and 'no-shame' activity (Genesis 2:25). We'll talk more about all this later.

Throughout the book you will find words that have been highlighted to look like **THIS**. Some of you may think you know what these words mean, but please read the description given in Part 2 of the book anyway.

You will also find 'Alert' stations sprinkled through the book. They will warn you about wrong ways of thinking and talking about sex, and about unhealthy and often dangerous sexual behaviours.

If you have experienced any of what we mention, don't hold it in. Speak to Mum, Dad, a trusted older person or teacher. Here's the first one:

Alert

Words for sex and sexual acts

Some girls and boys use ugly and insulting words to describe genital parts and sexual activity. Why would anyone take a gift from God and make it a swear word? It's an awful thing to do.

Mostly they don't understand the meaning of the terms they use; they've picked them up from someone else, usually an older brother, sister or adult. Sometimes from a TV show. Don't repeat these as swear words. They're not funny—just silly. Ask Mum, Dad or another trusted adult what the word means. They will explain it to you even if they blush and stutter while doing it!

In this book, you will learn to use the correct words for parts of the body and for sexual acts. At the end of this book, you will be able to discuss God's wonderful gift of your sexual body in a good, clean and healthy way.

Now you know the different things people mean when they use the word 'sex'. But where does sex fit into God's plan for you, your family, friends and the world?

One place to get information is Mum and Dad. Throughout the book, you will find conversation starter boxes called 'Ask Mum and Dad'. Go on—talk to them. Some of you may be totally comfortable in doing so. Others may cringe at the thought of having 'the sex talk' with your parents! Don't worry. They most likely gave you the book to read! And they are waiting for you to come to them.

Here's the first one.

 ## Ask Mum & Dad

1 | When you were growing up, what did you believe sex meant?

2 | Who did you talk to about it? Did they teach you about sex at school? Or at church? What about your parents? Did they talk about sex openly?

Now we move to what God says about sex. And yes, the place we go to find that out is the Bible.

Did you ever wonder if the Bible has anything to say about sex? Let's find out together.

Does God have a plan for sex?

Sex was an important part of God's plan right from creation. Are you surprised to learn that?

We read about this in Genesis chapters 1 and 2—the very first chapters of the first book of the Bible. Let's look at it together.

> Then God said, 'Let us make mankind in our image, in our likeness, so that they may rule over the fish in the sea and the birds in the sky, over the livestock and all the wild animals, and over all the creatures that move along the ground'. So God created mankind in his own image, in the image of God he created them; male and female he created them. God blessed them and said to them, 'Be fruitful and increase in number; fill the earth and subdue it'. (Genesis 1:26–28)

> … that is why a man leaves his father and mother and is united to his wife, and they become one flesh. Adam and his wife were both naked, and they felt no shame. (Genesis 2:24–25)

We know that this is God's plan for sexuality because later, in the New Testament, Jesus himself goes back to both these passages when asked about marriage and divorce (in Matthew 19:4–5). Later, the Apostle Paul refers to Genesis 2:24–25 when talking about marriage (Ephesians 5:31).

In the creation story, we see the three aspects of sex we talked about a moment ago.

1 | Sex as gender: God made humans as male and female.

2 | Sexual bodies: God made our bodies so that we could come together as male and female to have babies and have fun while doing it.

3 | Sexual activity: God wanted Adam and Eve to come together as 'one flesh'. This means God intended sex to be something that a man and a woman enjoy together, in a special relationship.

We also see a fourth aspect of sexuality—one that people don't usually talk about. That's a pity, because it's actually the one that ties it all together.

4 | Sex in the unique relationship of marriage: one where the man leaves his parents and unites with a woman in marriage. When God brought Adam and Eve together, he set the pattern and place for sex—marriage.

Let's talk for a while about each of these four aspects of sex.

Sex as gender: created as man and woman

 **Think spot**

What makes you a girl or a boy?

Let's forget for a moment about the genital bits (penis and scrotum for boys, and vulva and vagina for girls). What else makes you a boy or girl? List these.

Do you understand? Being a boy or girl is about your genitals, but it's a lot more than that—it's a whole person thing.

To be a human being is to be either a boy or a girl—male or female. This is your 'gender'. It was decided the moment you were formed. It happened when your parents had sexual intercourse and Dad's sperm (carrying either an X or a Y **CHROMOSOME**) met Mum's egg (carrying an X chromosome). An XX combination and you were a girl; an XY and you were a boy. You didn't choose which one you would be. Neither did your mum and dad. Only God knew. And you'll be that boy or girl who grows up to be a man or woman for the rest of your life. You can't suddenly decide that you want to change from one to the other. It doesn't work that way.

The pattern for gender was set in the Garden of Eden. Adam was completely male. His body was male and he knew he was a male. He also recognised that he would behave in the way that men should and he fell crazily in love with Eve. Similarly Eve was a complete woman from her head to her toes.

We see this male–female sex difference today. Look around you. Being a boy or a girl is simple, right? Blue booties for a boy and pink for a girl. Most little boys play with trucks and run around in superhero T-shirts. And most girls play with dolls and run around with fairy wings and nail polish. There's Dad, Uncle and Gramps, Mum, Aunty and Grandma—all clearly male and female. You've probably never stopped to think about this. They just are.

Let's go back to the Genesis story. It goes on to tell us how Adam and Eve (our first father and mother) refused to obey God. They decided that they could run their lives without him. Because they disobeyed God, they had to leave the Garden of Eden (Genesis 3). Their perfect lives, including their relationships with God and each other, were spoiled. One of the things that got messed up was the perfection of their maleness and femaleness.

This continues today. Men and women don't live as God tells them to in the Bible. And so our lives are not healthy and happy like God intended for us—we're all messed up. Sometimes, people are sexually attracted to someone of the same sex (this is called **HOMOSEXUALITY** as opposed to boy–girl attraction which is called heterosexuality). And rarely, a boy may even think he is really a girl or the other way round (called gender identity problems, gender dysphoria or **TRANSGENDER**). Sometimes even the way the genitals form in the womb goes wrong and we have babies born with genitals that don't look clearly boy or girl (called **INTERSEX**).

Alert

Homosexuality and bullying

True homosexuality (being sexually attracted to someone of the same sex—boy to boy or girl to girl) is rare: about 3-4% of all people. Gender identity problems are even rarer: about one in several thousand people.

Sometimes girls and boys call each other homosexuals to tease and bully. They usually don't say 'homosexual' but use 'gay' or some other insulting term. This is wrong and very hurtful. It's not funny to make a joke of someone's sexuality or to use these terms as an insult.

If you've had someone call you by such a word, or seen it happen in the playground, don't ignore it. Talk to a teacher or Mum and Dad.

We talk more about homosexuality in Part 2, so you can go there now if you'd like to know more about this and then come back to here.

Sexual bodies: created to come together to make babies

In Genesis 1, God made humans 'male and female', and told them to 'be fruitful and increase in number'. So one reason God made humanity as male and female was because he wanted our bodies to work together to make babies. This is the biological purpose for having sexual parts. But God also meant for this coming together as man and woman to be about more than just having babies; he wanted it to be a special act of **INTIMACY** between two people. We'll discuss the importance of this later, when we talk about the significance of marriage.

When it comes to our bodies (our muscles and blood vessels, and all that), boys and girls are actually almost the same. The sexual parts of our bodies are the big exception.

 **Think spot**

The sexual parts of your body

We will be talking more about the parts of your body and the changes that take place in the next chapter of the book. But for now, write down what you think are the special parts of your body that make you a girl or a boy.

God designed our sexual biology so that when a man and a woman come together and have sex, their bodies work together really well. It is God's design; therefore, sex is not silly or stupid—it's special.

This means the sexual parts of our bodies are a good thing. And the changes that will take place in your body as you go through puberty are good changes. It may feel strange; you may not really understand what's happening to you. That's OK. God knows what's happening to you. The Bible says he put you together in your mother's womb (Psalm 139:13-16). Imagine that! God planned what you would be like from the time you were just a single cell—so tiny you could fit on the tip of a needle! If God guided you through those very first days of your existence, he can take care of you through puberty.

The Bible tells us that the body parts that we feel a little shy about are actually special. Speaking to a group of Christians in Corinth (1 Corinthians 12:21-23), the Apostle Paul says that the parts of our body that we don't put on display and fuss over (our sexual bits!) are actually the ones we should treat carefully—even giving them special honour.

Some of you might have started noticing changes in your body, both in your sexual bits and the rest of it. Accept and celebrate what's happening—it's God's way of getting you ready to be a man or a woman. Or you may not have started on the journey yet. That's OK too—everyone is different. God is in control and he has a particular purpose for the grown-up you. He'll get you there at just the right time.

Sexual activity: God's purpose for sex

Do you know a (boy or girl) you consider really cute? Do you ever imagine yourself with that person, holding their hand or kissing them? These are the early rumblings of your emotional brain waking up to sexual feelings, and these thoughts are absolutely normal.

Or maybe you have absolutely no interest in the other sex. You might think that boys are a pain or that girls are totally boring. As for sex—that's so gross! Why would you even think about it? If this is you, it means that your sex hormones haven't switched on your sexual feelings yet. This too is normal.

We've already mentioned the term 'sexual activity' several times and you may not be sure exactly what this means. Let's clear that up now.

 **Alert**

Sexual activity

What are the things that a boy and a girl can do together? Write down *whatever* comes to mind.

Now go back over the list and pick out ones that you think are 'sexual' in any way.

What made you choose some things as 'sexual activities'?

What makes an activity 'sexual' is the *meaning* the boy and girl give to it and how they *feel* when they are doing it.

You learn meanings from people around you—from your family and culture. Feelings are in your mind. So holding hands may be just an act of friendship to some people, but others may consider it a sexual activity. Or take kissing. Your little brother or sister may kiss you on your mouth, and that would be OK—even cute. But if a boy or girl your age or older kissed you on the mouth, that would mean something different.

This may sound confusing right now; don't worry. We'll come back to this later in the book.

While many activities may give us a sexual feeling, anything that involves the sexual parts (genitals) is special. God didn't just make the sexual parts of our bodies; he wants us to use them—at the right time. And that right time is when our bodies have fully developed, and when we're in the right relationship for sex: marriage.

In the Genesis story, we hear God telling Adam and Eve to 'be fruitful and increase in number; fill the earth and subdue it'. Fruitfulness here involves having babies. In order to make babies the woman needs to get pregnant. And to get pregnant, the husband and wife need to make love (have sexual intercourse).

Do you see? God planned sexual activity right from creation. It's not 'bad' or 'dirty'. It's certainly not 'sinful'—not the way God intended it to be, anyway. It's part of the way God made us; it's a good gift from God, meant to make us happy and healthy.

Look again at the story in Genesis. It places sexual activity in a particular setting: one man (Adam the husband) and one woman (Eve the wife) coming together in a loving and trusting (a 'naked and no-shame') relationship of marriage. In this coming together sexually, there will be the chance of making a baby (procreation) and having fun too.

All this talk about sex might be grossing you out. That's OK. Your body and brain probably aren't ready for it yet, but one day they will be. The sexual parts of your body will develop, and you'll start having sexual feelings. Just because you have sexual feelings doesn't mean you have to do something about them. You should wait until you are ready—not just ready in terms of the biology of your body and brain, but in terms of the right time and place for sexual activity.

Most of you will meet someone of the opposite gender whom you will marry. That'll be the right time to have sex because your brain, body and relationship will all be ready. Until that time, it is best to control your sexual feelings and enjoy close friendships with boys and girls (be intimate with them without having sex). Some may actually live this way as single men and women all their lives. This too is OK.

This is God's plan for sexual activity: it is a gift and a blessing to be used and enjoyed in marriage. Remember, when God created Adam and Eve and brought them together as husband and wife, he 'saw all that he had made, and *it was very good*' (Genesis 1:31).

 ## Ask Mum & Dad

1 | Do you remember what age you were when you were first interested in sex?

2 | When and where did you learn about sex as a gift from God?

3 | How did you relate to other boys and girls when you were growing up? How were you able to have intimate friendships, especially with those of the opposite sex, without it becoming sexual?

Sex and relationships: why marriage is important

The Bible says that sexual activity, especially those that involve the sexual parts of the body (genitals), is for marriage. This is different to the way the world thinks about sex. In today's world, sex is everywhere. 'Everybody's doing it.'

Many of you may have read about sex in magazines, heard about sexual acts in the words of pop songs, or watched them in movies or music videos. Perhaps you've seen sexy photos or sexual acts on videos or the internet. Your reaction to these may have been one of 'shock-horror' or mild interest. Perhaps you and your friends have talked about it.

There are two messages you will hear from society:

(i) *'Sexual activity makes you feel good. And if something feels good, then you should just do it.'*

Sexual activity feels good because God gives us a brain chemistry that makes sexual activity exciting and fun. However, just because something feels good does not make it good for you! You may feel good while eating a whole tub of ice-cream, but the chances are that you will be sick soon after. You practise self-control when eating ice-cream. You don't eat the whole tub; just a bowlful. And you eat it at the right time: at the end of the meal, after eating healthy food for a main course. It's even more important to practise self-control in sex, because sex involves your deepest emotions and the most special parts of your body.

Sex in marriage is like ice-cream for dessert: something really nice to look forward to as part of a good, healthy meal. Sex outside marriage is like trying to eat only ice-cream, all the time, for breakfast, lunch and dinner. You might feel good while you're eating it, but you'll get very sick, very quickly.

Is it any wonder that celebrities and pop stars who 'just do it' are so messed up?

 **Alert**

Sexual activity outside of marriage

Based on the messages you hear from the media, magazines and your friends, why do people have sex outside of marriage?

If you and your friends have talked about it, what words and phrases have you heard used? Do you think these are good and healthy words to use?

Alert

Sex and the media

Some of you may find the sexual images and words in music videos and TV shows and on the internet disturbing and upsetting. This sort of 'in your face' sex is given the name '**PORNOGRAPHY**'.

Don't just ignore these feelings. Firstly, stop! Don't continue watching it. If you are with friends, it's OK to walk away or say that you don't want to see it. Secondly, talk to someone like Mum, Dad, another trusted adult or teacher about it and how seeing these images made you feel. We discuss this more in Part 2 of the book.

(ii) *'If you are in love with someone, and you both want it—it's OK to make love.'*

The phrase 'make love' usually means to have sexual intercourse. Some girls and boys think that if you say you are 'in love' with someone then you must 'make love' to them.

What does it mean to be 'in love'?

When you were little you may have loved your Barbie® doll or video game. That's not being 'in love'. Neither is the love you feel for your best friend.

Think spot

What makes your friendship with your best friend ('bestie') special? Write it down.

What did you write down?

Maybe you said that you would help them or 'be there' for them at all times—during the good times when they are being nice to you, and at the not-so-good times when they are being a pain! You support friends when they are in trouble, even if it costs you time, energy, money, or you miss out on doing something else. And they would do the same for you.

This is being a good friend.

Then there are the passing crushes. As your sexual brain wakes up, you may start to get sexual feelings for a particular person of the opposite sex, even the same sex. Sometimes it is a crush on a person you admire, like a sportsperson or pop star. This person may never know you even exist, but you admire them from a distance. It's a one-way relationship and passes in a while.

Other times you get a crush on someone you know. You want to be with this person as much as possible; you think about them all the time and feel excited when you see them or they notice you. These feelings are caused by brain chemicals (mainly one called dopamine, which is well-named given that being in love is such a dopey feeling!) At this stage of your life, you will go through times of feeling this way about a person, and then in a few months wonder what you saw in him or her!

Don't take these feelings too seriously. Definitely don't act on them by being sexually active with the person you have a crush on. When you get over the feelings, you'll feel bad. And you might have done or said something that you regret, but what's done is done; you'll never be able to take it back.

This 'falling in love' feeling is a sign that your brain is getting ready for what the Bible calls a 'one flesh' relationship (Genesis 2:24)—when you will meet and marry someone of the opposite sex. You will be *in love* but also *be loved by* your husband or wife. The important thing is that marriage is far more than two people being 'in love' with each other. It is about two people making promises to love and care for each other for as long as they live—no matter what happens or how old they get—and to continue to do so long after the crazy 'in love' feelings are gone.

It's like how God loves his children—the Church. Jesus showed us how to do it. Jesus is God's love. Jesus is God loving us even when we turn away from him and refuse to obey him. Here are a couple of famous verses from the Bible:

> *For God so loved the world that he gave his one and only Son, that whoever believes in him shall not perish but have eternal life.* (John 3:16)

> *God demonstrates his own love for us in this: While we were still sinners, Christ died for us.* (Romans 5:8)

That is an amazing love! The creator of the universe forgave us and promised us heaven even though we turned away from him. That's the love God wants us to share as husband and wife in marriage.

That's why the traditional Christian wedding ceremony includes language like this:

> 'For better or worse, for richer or poorer, in sickness and in health',

> 'With all that I am, and all that I have, I honour you'.

In marriage, a man and a woman promise to be there for each other, and care for each other, for the rest of their lives. They promise to love each other, and put the other person's needs first, in everything—including sex. Marriage holds all the other aspects of sex together. In a marriage, a man and a woman (sex as gender), whose bodies and brains have developed into sexual maturity (sex as physical development) enter into a special relationship that involves, among other things, having sex with each other (sex as activity).

When I counsel married couples who have relationship problems, often one or both of them admit they had sex before (with each other or someone else), or outside of their marriage. And now they're full of sadness and regret. These problems happen when people believe that they can improve on God's pattern for life. Instead of following God's advice, we do what we think is right—what we desire.

That's why we urge you to wait. Don't give away God's good gift of sex; keep it for where God planned it to be enjoyed—in a loving marriage.

Ask Mum & Dad

1 | If you're a girl, ask Mum; if you're a boy, ask Dad: How is your love for your wife/husband different from the love you feel for your friends?

2 | Where and when did you learn about marriage?

Whether you were born a boy or a girl, the sexual parts of your body and all of your sexual feelings are gifts from God—gifts that he wants you to use at the right time: when you are married.

In the next chapters we will look in more detail at these changes in your body and brain, and what they mean to you as a Christian boy or girl.

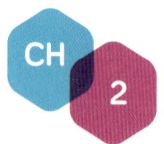

Your body: different and special

Look around you. What sorts of images of bodies do you see on TV, the internet, billboards and in magazines? Are they slightly lumpy bodies with pimples and crooked teeth? Of course not! They are beautiful people with perfect bodies.

What message do these images communicate? They tell girls that they should be thinner, sexier, hotter, or whatever. They must have great boobs, flawless skin and perfect hair. And what do boys hear? They should be taller and muscular in all the right places.

How many real people actually look or act like this ideal boy or girl?

Think spot

What do real people look like? Make a list of three adults and three friends around your age.

Based on the images you see of men and women in the media (TV, magazines, videos and movies) and on the internet, how would you rate their body, face, teeth, skin and hair? Give each person a score of '5' if they are just like the media images and '1' if they are only a little alike. How did they score?

I would be surprised if anyone on your list averaged above a score of three!

Why are real-life bodies so unlike what we see in the media?

This is because the people photographed are models. They spend a lot of their time and money making their bodies look good for photographs and film. In addition to this, celebrities' photographs are changed by computer 'enhancement' (that is, programs such as Adobe PhotoShop® are used to take out wrinkles, spots and blemishes—they make hips and thighs thinner and breasts and lips plumper). Many of the models and movie stars have had plastic surgery; some skinny ones have eating disorders; and some muscular men are on drugs like steroids that also ruin their health. In other words: those bodies aren't real. They're fake.

It's not fair to compare ourselves with them. It's like trying to play sport against someone who cheats all the time. Of course you're going to lose: they're not playing fair. So don't feel bad that your body doesn't look like what you see on TV or the internet. Don't waste your time feeling sad or angry that you don't have what the celebrities have. Real, healthy bodies are beautiful. Enjoy what you do have, and thank God for it.

Further, the images of what is considered a beautiful body change with time. What was considered cute and sexy in your parents' day may be very different to what you now consider to be amazing. It is also different across cultures. What is considered beautiful in Western cultures is different to that in India or China or many other places.

Ask Mum & Dad

1 | When you were young, what was considered the ideal body for women and men?

2 | Where did you get this information from?

Chances are that, just when you feel somewhat comfortable with your body, things will start to change. Your breasts, genitals and general body shape alter. Acne appears and you develop body hair. Even your voice sounds different.

Some of you may be OK with the changes—perhaps your mum and dad, teachers or other adults have discussed these with you. For others, the body changes might be uncomfortable—even a little scary. Perhaps all the information you have is based on playground talk and what's happening to your friends. You might feel confused and need more help.

To add to the changes you can see, your brain feels like it's on a roller-coaster. Sometimes you want to climb into your mum's lap and cry your heart out. At other times you think that Mum and Dad are such losers. And your friends seem to be just as clueless as you are.

And then there's sex. You may get thoughts and feelings about yourself and about other people around you. Funny thoughts about touching, hugging and even kissing someone pop into your head. It's embarrassing and sometimes downright creepy. Or maybe your friends talk about sex and boyfriends and girlfriends, but you feel nothing: You think: 'What's with the sex thing?' So, you might be wondering whether you're weird or something.

Your parents might be trying to talk to you about sex, but it's just embarrassing and gross. So you don't listen, or say you're not ready. You might say that you have already learned about sex at school when actually all you know comes from magazines, your friends and sometimes photos or videos on the internet.

Things to remember

- You are special to God!

    » He made you, and is watching over you (Psalm 139).

    » Jesus came and died for you. Every part of you is special and this includes your body. Your body is precious to God. So use it to honour him (1 Corinthians 6:15a, 19–20).

- Your body and brain are a work in progress.

    » Your sexual body: You are changing from a child to an adult but no two boys or girls develop in the same way or at the same pace. Everyone is different and it's all normal. So don't stress.

    » Your sexual brain: Some boys and girls start thinking sexual thoughts at eight and nine years of age; others don't until their mid-teens. A few don't care about sex at all. Again, everyone is different and it's all normal. Don't stress.

- Whatever your body looks like and however confused your brain feels right now, God loves you, and so do your parents and family and church.

- A healthy body image is important. How you see your own body, and how you present yourself to others, not only matters to you, it matters to your parents and to God.

A body that's special to God

As a Christian boy or girl, God made you in his image (Genesis 1:26–27) and you're his child (Romans 8:14–15). This means that *every* part of your body is special—just the way it is right now. Remember we said that the parts of the body we are most shy about are given special honour (1 Corinthians 12:21–23)? This means that at your age, the parts that are most honoured are the ones that are changing and developing!

God also knows every little change that is taking place in your body (Psalm 139:13–16). His opinion matters more than anyone else's. God doesn't care about how thin, fat, tall or small you are—not even how smart you are. You are special just as you are. That's why you can love your body and all the changes taking place in it.

God also knows every thought and feeling you have (Psalm 139:1–3). He knows when you can't make up your mind over something, and he knows when you turn away from good advice and choose to do something crazy. The wonderful thing is: God is always there to forgive you and lead you back to the right way. He does this through his words in the Bible (Hebrews 4:12) and through your parents' guidance (Proverbs 4).

Stand in front of a mirror. Have a good look at yourself—your face, chest, stomach, hands and feet. Now speak to your image; tell yourself that God loves you just the way you are. And he will continue to love you through all the changes in your body.

These Bible verses may also help you:

> *I praise you because I am fearfully and wonderfully made; your works are wonderful, I know that full well.* (Psalm 139:14)

> *Do you not know that your bodies are members of Christ himself? Do you not know that your bodies are temples of the Holy Spirit, who is in you, whom you have received from*

God? You are not your own; you were bought at a price. Therefore honour God with your bodies. (1 Corinthians 6:15a, 19–20)

Being sure of God's love for you means that you can be free to be who you are, because in God's eyes *you are special*.

A body that's changing

Sadly, many boys and girls your age are not happy with their bodies.

As doctors we find that even by age six little girls and boys start worrying about their bodies. By 12 and 13 years of age many girls and boys are concerned about their body shape, weight and general body structure: breasts and pubic area for girls, and muscles, penis and scrotum for boys. We are finding more and more children suffering from what are called eating disorders—trying to become skinnier by starving themselves or making themselves vomit. Some boys even take drugs to build muscles. They only succeed in making themselves sick and messing up their bodies.

You may not be like this. You may be totally confident that God loves you just as you are, and that your parents and family and friends do too. You know what changes to expect. But look around you. Some of your friends and schoolmates will be unhappy with how they look. Some may even be getting bullied for being different in some way.

This part of this book will explain the changes that happen in your body as you grow up from being a child to being a young adult. It will help you to understand what's happening, and will continue to happen, in your body. It will also help you to understand why you and some of your friends could feel anxious about these changes.

It will also teach you a whole lot of new terms you can use to impress your science and PDHPE teachers!

Words you need to know

PUBERTY: This is a word coming from the Latin, *pubertas*, meaning 'the virile age'. Puberty is the beginning of what we call sexual maturity. It refers to all the changes in your body that take you from being a child to a young person capable of having sex and making a baby.

MENARCHE: The first menstrual period in a girl is the event that marks the start of puberty in a girl. Actually many changes would already have happened in the body before **MENARCHE**. The onset of menstrual periods signals that a girl is producing eggs (or ova) and it's possible for her to become pregnant if she has sexual intercourse. If you'd like to know more about menstruation, go to Part 2—Menarche.

SPERMARCHE: The time in a boy when the testes produce sperm. It is signalled by the first **EJACULATION**. This is usually noticed by a boy when he has a '**WET DREAM**'. The term 'spermarche' is rarely used. This is probably because it is not as memorable an event as menarche (except to the individual boy of course). A boy is now able to get a girl pregnant if he has sexual intercourse with her. If you'd like to know more about wet dreams or ejaculations, look for these topics in Part 2.

ADOLESCENCE: This is a longer period than puberty. It is the time between puberty and becoming an adult. The word comes from the Latin, *adolescere*, which means 'to grow' or 'to develop towards maturity'.

Hormones direct changes in your body

There is a biological clock deep in your brain in an area called the hypothalamus. This is where it all starts. About a year before you actually see any changes in your body, the hypothalamus starts making a chemical called gonadotropin-releasing hormone (GnRH). Now that's a term you can use to impress your Science teacher!

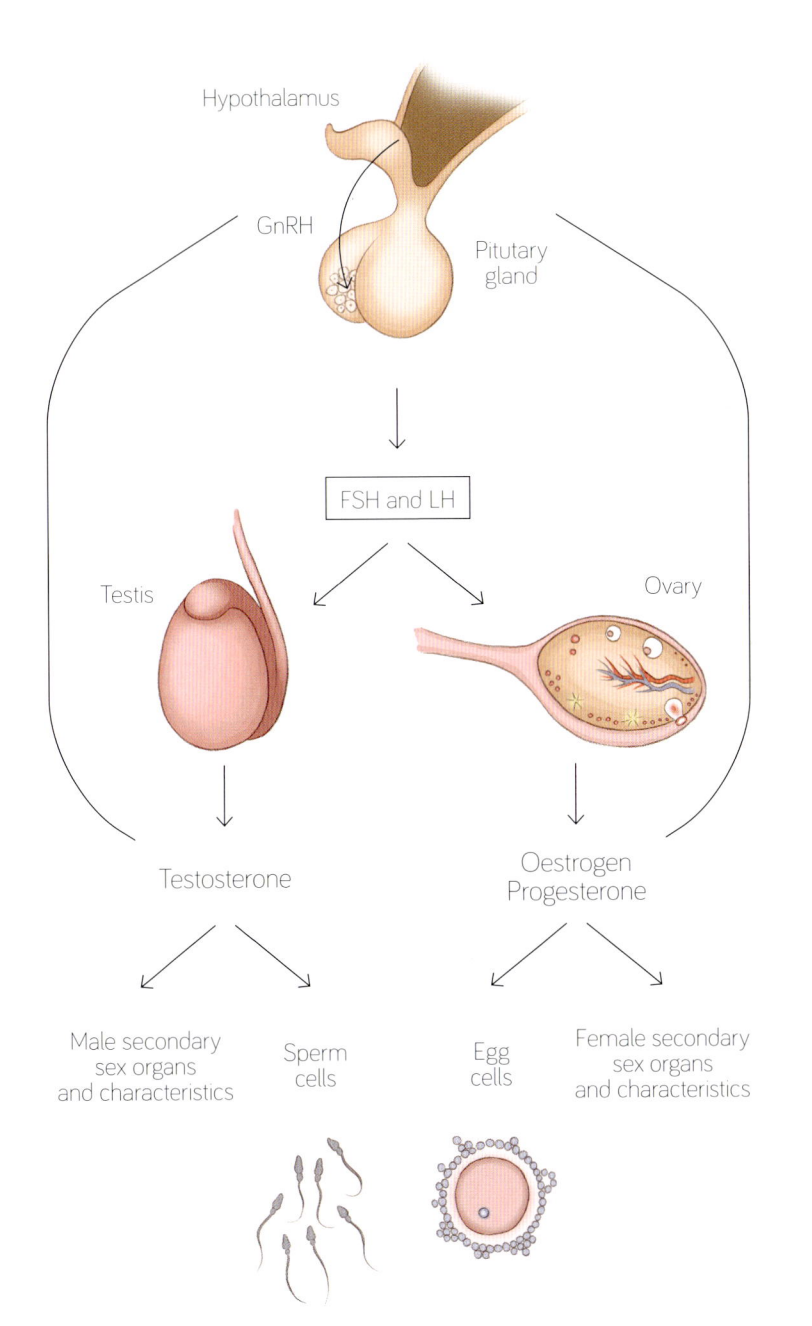

```
Hypothalamus
   │
 GnRH
   ↓
Pituitary gland
   │
   ↓
FSH and LH
   ↙        ↘
Testis      Ovary
  ↓           ↓
Testosterone  Oestrogen
              Progesterone
  ↙    ↘      ↙       ↘
Male      Sperm   Egg    Female
secondary cells   cells  secondary
sex organs               sex organs
and characteristics      and characteristics
```

Your body: different and special

GnRH races down to a little pea-shaped structure attached to your brain, called the pituitary gland. It causes the release of other chemicals called gonadotropins (luteinizing hormone [LH] and follicle-stimulating hormone [FSH]). The word 'gonad' refers to the sex gland (testes if a boy and ovaries if a girl). The word 'trophic' means to make active. That is what the LH and FSH do: they wake up your sex glands.

Once woken up, testes start producing sperms and they will continue to do so until you move from being a boy to an adult and into old age. Once a girl's ovaries wake up, they produce roughly one egg a month until a time called menopause (somewhere between 50 and 60 years old). The gonads also produce increasing amounts of sex hormones (oestrogen if you are a girl and testosterone if you are a boy).

The rest of your 'child body' now gets the message that it's time to start the changes that will make you grow into a sexually mature adult.

You are now biologically ready to enter the world of sexual reproduction. This doesn't happen overnight; it can start anytime between seven and 12 years of age. The pace at which changes take place also varies for each boy and girl. And you probably won't reach your adult size and shape until you are 20. So don't be impatient if nothing has happened to you yet.

So, what should you expect to see happen when your body does wake up sexually?

Body changes at puberty

Here are some general facts about the body and changes at puberty. You may have heard about these in school or from your parents, but read on anyway. You will probably learn something new.

1 | Both boys and girls go through a growth spurt. You get taller and your body shape changes. Boys get more muscular and girls get

curvier. You also start noticing skin changes with growth of underarm hair and pimples (acne).

2 | There are changes inside the body, in what is called the internal genitalia, designed to get these parts ready for sexual activity. If you are a girl, a hormone called oestrogen will make your womb (uterus) increase in size, so it will be ready to accept and grow a baby. If you are a boy, the tubes and other glands such as the prostate get ready to nourish the developing sperm and guide it out of the body. The outward sign that this is happening is the event of menarche (first menstrual period) for the girl and erections and ejaculations for the boy.

3 | There are also visible changes called the secondary sexual characteristics. These are the ones you notice most. In girls it is about breast development, vulva (labia major, labia minor and clitoris) enlargement and pubic hair growth. In boys the testicular sac called the scrotum enlarges and gets wrinkled and hairy. The penis lengthens and thickens and may get darker in colour. At about this time boys also find that, driven by testosterone, their voices change and eventually get deeper.

What you may not know or have understood, is that there is a big variation between any two girls or boys in the way that this growth takes place. The timing of the changes and how fast each part of the body develops varies from person to person.

Yes, every one of you is different.

Why does this happen? Why don't all boys and girls develop at the same rate and end up in the same place?

Boys, girls and individual differences

As we said, the hormone-driven body developments that take place in puberty in your breasts, vulva, penis and pubic hair are given the term 'secondary sexual characteristics'. This is because they are 'second' to the genital differences between boys and girls at birth.

Remember we said that every one of you is different in how you grow and develop? Why is that?

Firstly, girls start off on their journey to maturity earlier than boys. Girls can start at seven or eight years of age whereas boys generally lag behind by a year or two. This varies from person to person—some girls may not start until they are 12 and some boys will start early at eight. So if as a girl you feel that the boys your age are underdeveloped, that's because they are, compared to you. The reverse holds for boys—they might notice growing breasts in the girls around them before they experience any change in themselves.

Secondly, it's about your family. Your body is influenced by what your parents looked like when they were your age! This is called genetics or heredity.

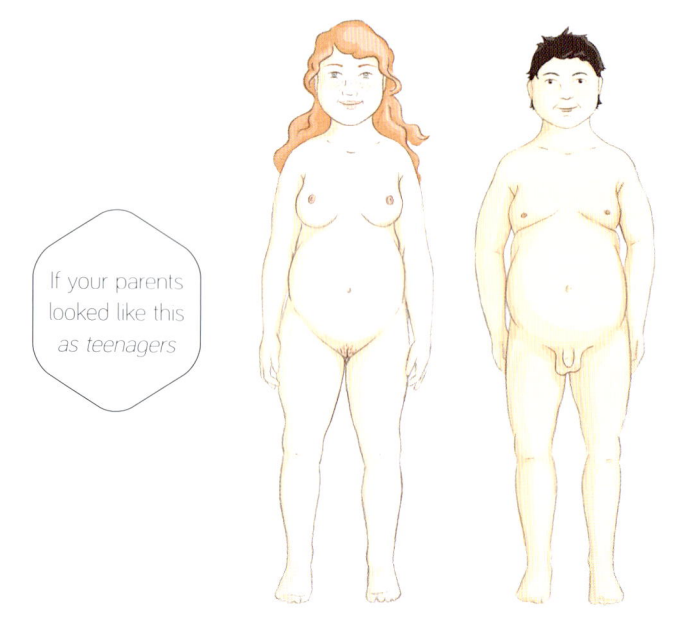

If your parents looked like this *as teenagers*

Or your parents looked like this *as teenagers*

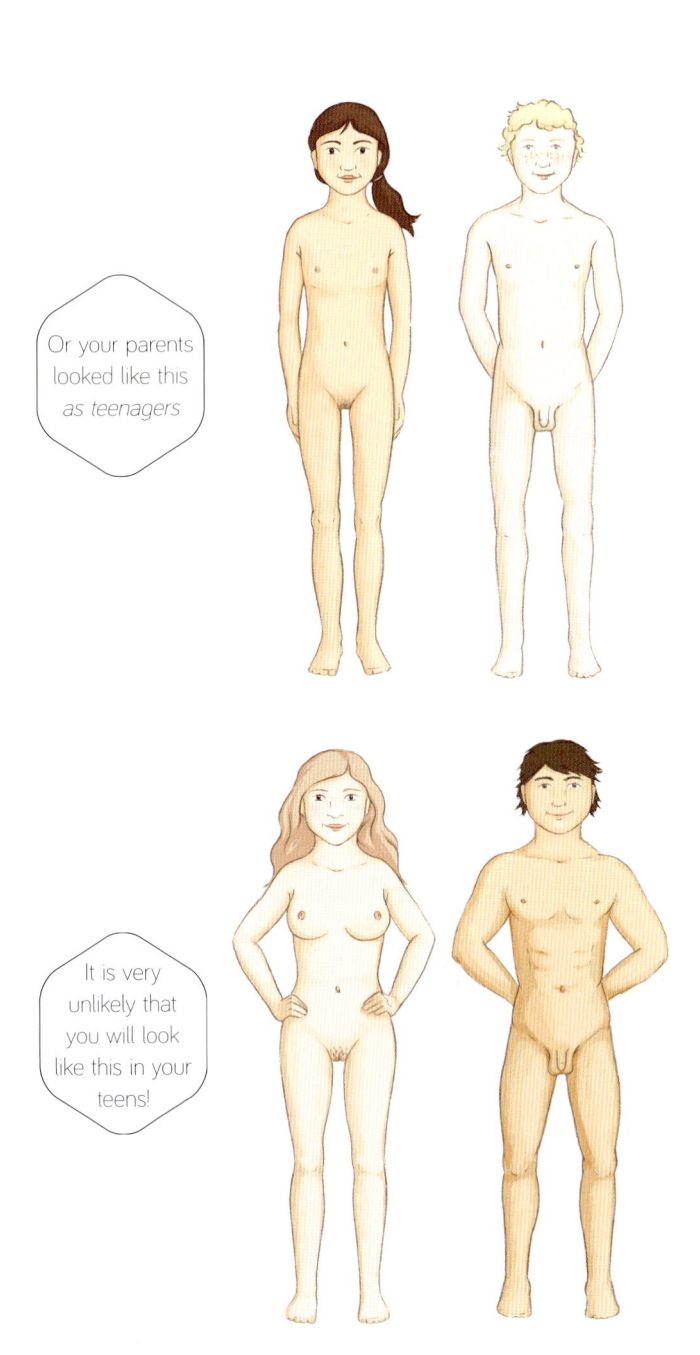

It is very unlikely that you will look like this in your teens!

Your body: different and special

31

Ask Mum & Dad

Ask your mum and dad to show you photos or videos of themselves at your age.

Discuss the ways in which you are like your mum and/or dad at the same age. These similarities (or differences) might be in how you look or how you behave (your personality).

You are meant to look at least in part like your parents. In the Bible we read that Adam fathered a son 'in his likeness', and named him Seth (Genesis 5:3).

Looking like and behaving like your parents is part of who you are.

These same family characteristics extend to *when* your body changes (breasts, pubic hair, vulva, penis and scrotum) start, and in fact where they finally end up! So look at some photos of what your parents or siblings looked like at your age—that's a far more realistic goal for your development than a photo from a magazine, the internet or a pop star in a music video.

You can however make some changes to your general body shape by eating well and exercising. Be careful here. We mean eating *well*, not starving yourself; exercising regularly, not becoming a 'gym junkie'. Never take dietary supplements or medicines to either lose weight or build up muscles. These chemicals disturb the natural growth processes in your body and you will end up being sick.

Finally, doctors are finding that the age at which puberty begins is getting earlier. We are not sure why this is. Researchers say it may be the chemicals and hormones in food and what we eat (our diet). At the other end, some girls who are in training for athletics or ballet and have a very low amount of body fat may not start puberty until their late teens.

Here's an activity for you to assess where you are in your puberty body change journey.

For girls: secondary sexual characteristics

We have discussed what happens in your body as you move from a child to a sexually mature adult. Now we're going to look specifically at two of these changes: breasts and pubic hair.

Breast development is usually the first sign of puberty in a girl and this may start anywhere from eight to 13 years old. The first thing you will notice is that the flat area around the nipple (areola) becomes enlarged and some firm tissue forms under the nipple. Pubic hair development follows soon after.

Below you'll see the five stages of breast development and pubic hair development[1]. Here's what we'd like you to do: on a piece of paper write down your current age and which developmental stage you think you are currently at. (If you like, you can come back to this book later and write the age you arrive at each of the stages.)

(i) Breasts

Stage 1: Childhood. The breasts have not started to develop. The breast tissue is flat on the chest and only the nipple is slightly raised.

Stage 2: A small flat button like mass of breast tissue develops under the nipple. This raises the nipple making it stick out a little from the chest. The ring of darker skin surrounding the nipple (called the areola) gets larger. You can feel the breast bud if you place your fingers flat on your chest.

---

1. These stages are based on 'Tanners stages' from: Marshall, WA & Tanner JM 1969, 'Variations in pattern of pubertal changes in girls', *Arch Dis Child*, 44, 235, pp. 291–303.

Stage 1

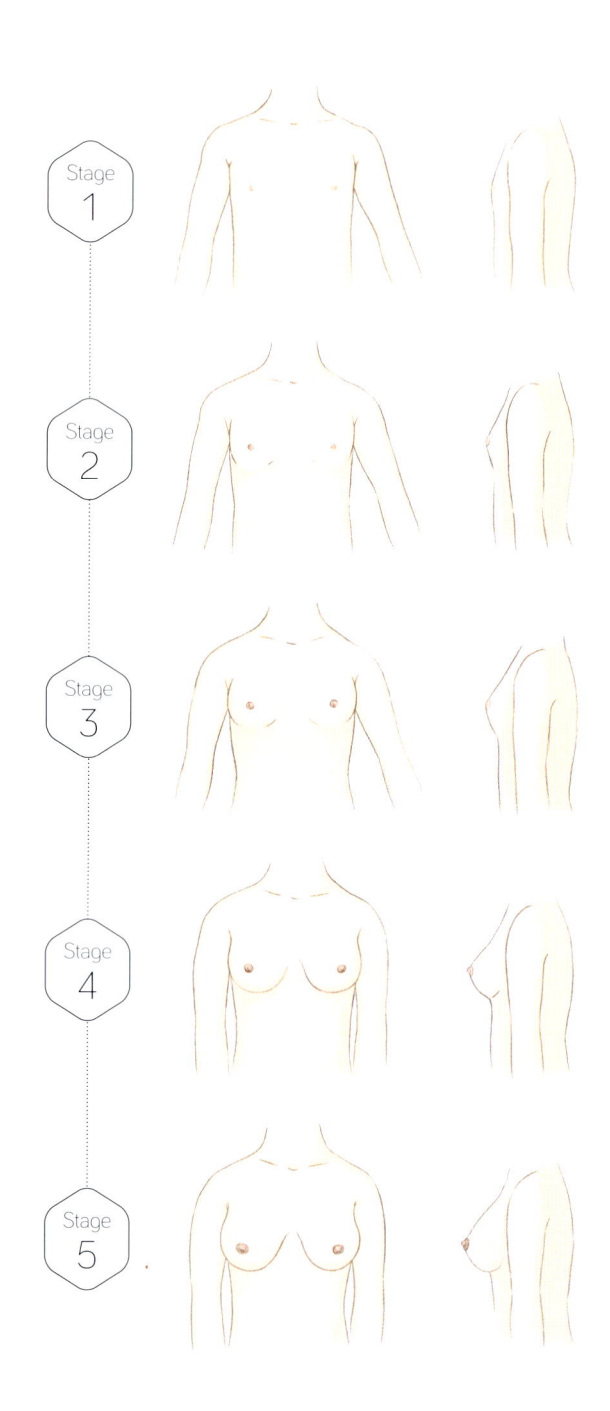

Stage 2

Stage 3

Stage 4

Stage 5

Stage 3: Breast development continues. More breast tissue develops and the areola and nipple also get larger. You can now recognise the breast shape.

Stage 4: The nipple and areola continue to grow and thicken in this stage. They may form a separate mound on the breast. The breast may take on a 'pointy' look.

Stage 5: The nipple and areola no longer form a separate mound. They merge into the breast contour. The size of the breast at this final stage can vary dramatically from a small 'AA' cup to a very generous 'J'.

Alert

Breast size and shape

It is important for both girls and boys to know that there is absolutely no relationship between breast size and how much a girl wants sex, how good she is as a lover, or even her ability to breastfeed a baby. Unfortunately, we live in a culture obsessed with breast size. It's driven by the sexualised images of large-breasted women in advertisements and pornography. Encouraged by the unnaturally large (often surgically enlarged) breasts on porn stars, some men of all ages 'perve' at girls with what they perceive as large breasts. If this is happening to you, then speak to your parents or a school counsellor.

God has given you the body you have. So enjoy being you! If you are shapely, don't pose and boast. Don't tease or bully others who are not like you. If, on the other hand, you are small-breasted, don't feel bad about it or allow what others say to get you down. You are beautiful in your own unique way—just as God planned it.

ii) Pubic hair

Read this description of the stages of **PUBIC** hair growth. Firstly, have a good look at yourself in front of a mirror. To do this, sit propped up in bed with your legs apart and knees bent. Use a small hand mirror to have a look at the area between your thighs called the vulva area or, more technically, your external genitals. This diagram shows you what an *adult* vulva looks like. Use the picture to locate the different parts of your genitals—remember that these are still developing and growing.

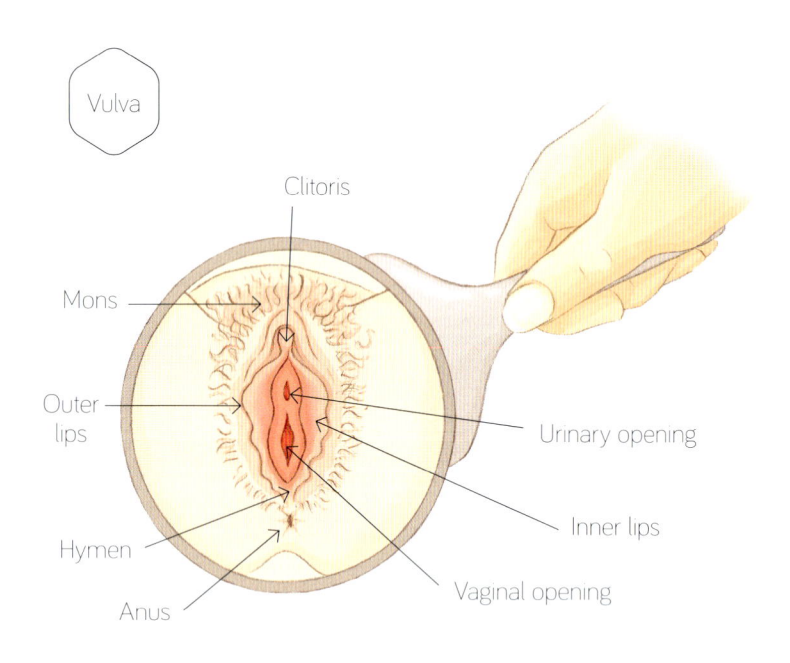

Vulva

Clitoris
Mons
Outer lips
Urinary opening
Inner lips
Hymen
Vaginal opening
Anus

Now take a look at the hair on your vulva and see what stage you might be at now.

Stage 1: This is the childhood stage. There may not be any hair or just some soft light hair like you have on your stomach area or arms. This is not pubic hair.

Stage 2: The pubic hair begins to appear, usually when you are between nine and 13 years of age. These first hairs may be straight or a bit curly. The exact colour and texture would depend on your ethnic group, but they will be a little rougher and maybe darker than the hair on your head or other parts of the body. They usually appear on the outer lips (called the labia major).

Stage 3: More hair grows on the outer lips and begins to grow on the mons area (see the diagram with the labels on page 36 if you're not sure where this is). There are more hairs at this stage and they may be thicker and rougher than before. This stage could last from two months to a couple of years.

Stage 4: There is now more hair; it is wiry and coarse, and extends over more of the mons. You might also notice the beginning of a triangular pattern of hair on the mons area. This stage also can last from a few months to a couple of years.

Stage 5: This is the adult stage. Your pubic hair will now be noticeably different in look and feel to the hair on other parts of your body, including your head hair. It is short, curly and coarse. If you are a blonde, the pubic hair is likely to be a darker shade. It takes the adult triangular pattern. In some girls it extends to the thighs and up a little way towards the umbilicus (your belly button)—this is normal too.

Having worked out where you are in terms of puberty development, put the paper away. You can come back to it in six months and see how much you have changed.

Stage 1

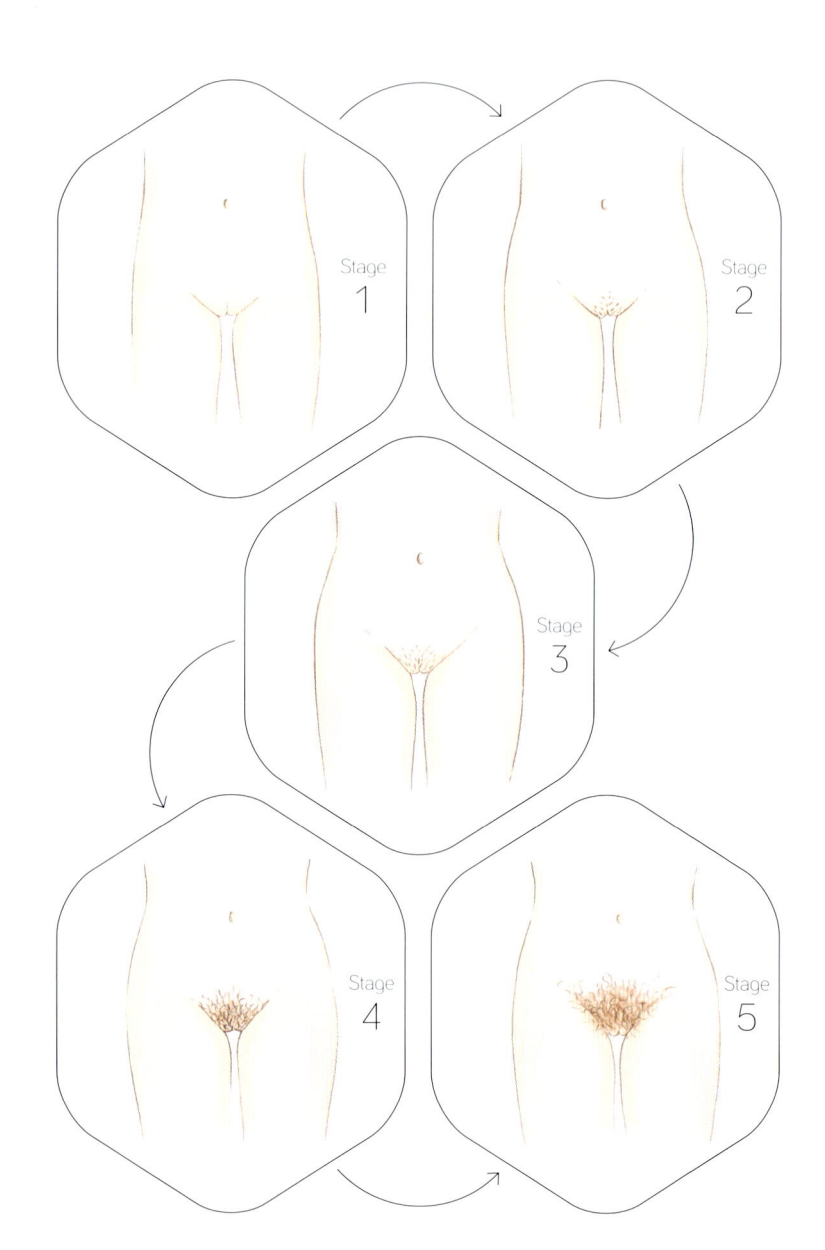

Stage 2

Stage 3

Stage 4

Stage 5

⚠ Alert

The myth of hairless genitals

Pubic hair is a normal part of growing up. However, advertising, social media and pornography tell us that to be sexually attractive, a girl needs to have a smooth, hairless pubic area. This is false, unnatural and unhealthy. You do not need to shave your pubic area, or have so-called beauty therapy treatments like **WAXING** or **LASER HAIR REMOVAL**—definitely not at your age, maybe not ever.

God has given you a beautiful body—love every bit of it. Don't try to change it to suit some unrealistic image driven by the media or **PORNOGRAPHY** or what your friends say is attractive.

For boys: secondary sexual characteristics

Boys (and men) of all ages are engrossed with their penis. It is common for boys to compare their penis size (even if it's just a sneaky look) in the locker room or toilets. So this activity may actually be more comfortable for you than it is for the girls.

In boys the external genitalia are the testes in the scrotal skin sac and the penis. Below we describe each of the five stages of external genital development and pubic hair growth that will take you from being a child to an adult. The picture on page 40 is that of an *adult* male genital area. Take a good look at your genitals in front of a full-length mirror and use the picture to identify the different parts. Feel your penis and scrotum. Your testes are soft almond-shaped structures inside your scrotum.

Pubic hair

Shaft

Male genitals

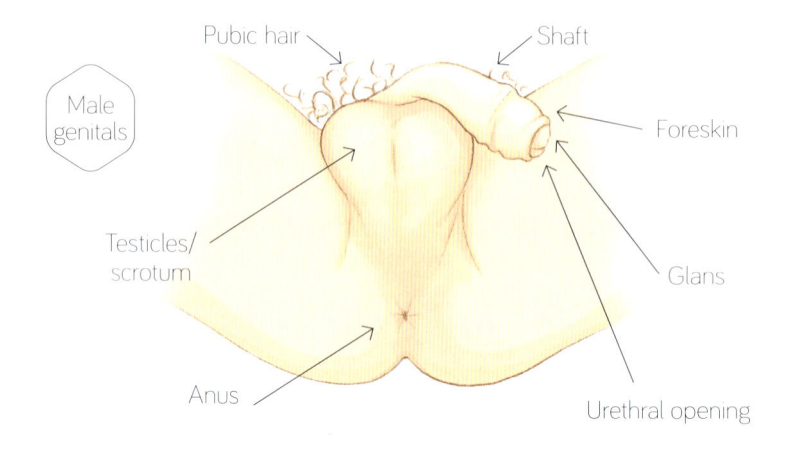

Foreskin

Testicles/ scrotum

Glans

Anus

Urethral opening

Here's what we'd like you to do: on a piece of paper write down your current age and which developmental stage you think you are currently at.[2] (If you like, you can come back to this book later and write the age you arrive at each of the stages.) Like the girls, you may find that you are at a different stage of external genital development and pubic hair growth than your friends or brothers. That is perfectly normal.

(i) External genitalia: testes, scrotum and penis

Stage 1: Childhood. You haven't started puberty. However, as your body grows generally the testes and penis may grow a little bit. The testes will be about 3 cm long. There will be no pubic hair.

Stage 2: The testes and scrotum begin to enlarge. Having testes of about 4 cm in length probably means you are at Stage 2. The scrotum, being the skin sac that holds the testes, now lengthens and hangs lower. The skin feels wrinkly and the testes slip around inside it. The

---

2. Tanner's stages for boys: Marshall WA, Tanner J, 1970 'Variations in the pattern of pubertal changes in boys', *Arch Dis Child*, No. 45, pp.13–23.

skin may be redder or darker in colour depending on your general skin colour. There may be a few pubic hairs at this stage (more on this later).

You may be anything from nine to 13 years old, or maybe even a little younger or older, when these changes start. This stage can last from a few months to a couple of years.

Stage 3: The penis gets longer. Yes, it's penis length, and not an increase in thickness, that you will notice first. The testes and scrotum continue to enlarge and deepen in colour and feel. This stage, like the earlier one, can last from a couple of months to over a year.

Stage 4: Thickening of the penis. The penis gets wider and the glans area becomes a separate area that you can detect. The scrotum and testes continue to grow and hang lower. There is usually pubic hair growth. Although generally seen in boys aged about 11 or 12 years, you may be ten or even 17 when you reach Stage 4.

Stage 5: The testes and scrotum are at an adult stage, as is the penis. Boys reach this final adult stage at about 16 years of age. But you could be as young as 13 or getting close to the end of your teens before your external genitals reach this adult appearance.

Alert

Masturbation

The word 'masturbation' is used to describe the act of touching the genitals for pleasure. The skin on the penis, especially at the tip (the area known as the glans), is very sensitive to touch. Therefore, picking up your penis either to urinate or wash it may feel good. This is normal. If something feels good, it is natural to want to explore and stay with that activity.

You will find that touching and rubbing your penis will make it get stiffer; this is because it fills with blood. This is called an **ERECTION**. At this stage of your growth, that's probably all that will happen. As your genitals grow some more, touching and stimulating the penis will lead to semen coming out. This is called an **EJACULATION**.

Touching yourself does not cause any illness in your brain or body. However it is not a healthy habit. The pleasure of sexual touch and the good feelings that go with it are a gift from God meant to be used in the one-flesh relationship of marriage.

So avoid doing it. If you find yourself spending a lot of time either masturbating or thinking about it, talk to Mum or Dad or another responsible adult.

We will discuss **MASTURBATION** in more detail in Part 2 of this book.

What is the normal adult structure of the penis and scrotum?

An average *adult penis at rest* is about 8 to 10 cm from tip to base. The testes in an adult are about 5 cm long and about 3 cm wide. It will take until the early 20s for a male penis to reach its adult potential. Even then, every man's penis is uniquely different in length, thickness and colour.

When a man is sexually excited, blood rushes into the penis and it enlarges in length and width. This is called an erection. The average length of an erect penis in an adult is about 12.5 to 15 cm—plenty long enough to function in sexual intercourse.

Stage 1

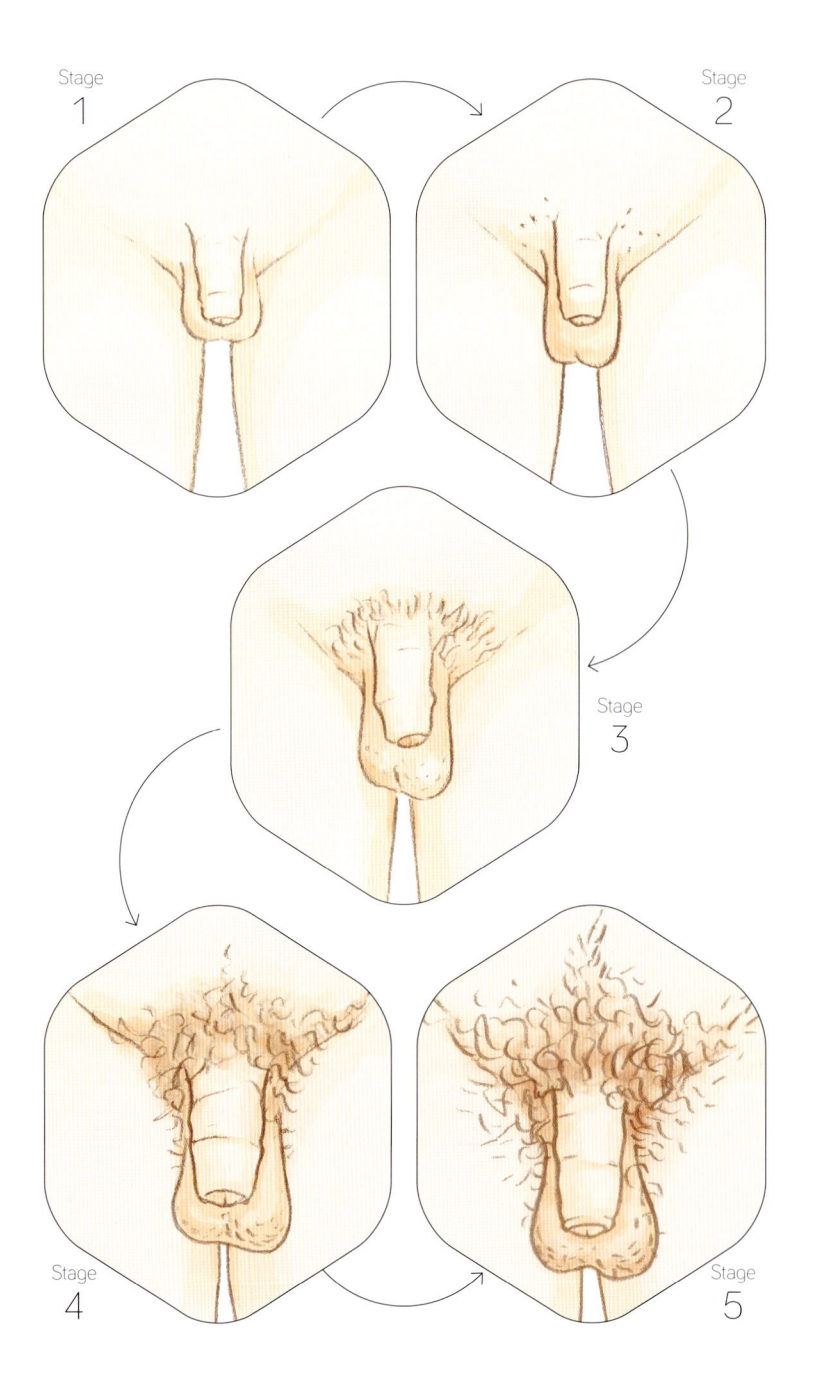

Stage 2

Stage 3

Stage 4

Stage 5

Your body: different and special

43

⚠ Alert

The myth of the large penis

For many boys and men, the size of their penis is very important; some even give their penis a name! Boys compare their penis sizes, and someone who moves slower through the stages of puberty as described above could be laughed at and bullied. This obsession with penis size is promoted by **PORNOGRAPHY**. In porn, men with impossibly huge penises make love to women for impossibly long spans of time. This is just *not* how things work in real life!

Why this obsession with penis size?

It's because many men assume that their sexual power determines their personal value. They think: large penis = sexually powerful = strong = worthwhile and valuable. Therefore: small penis = sexually weak = weak = worthless.

This of course is nonsense. There is no relationship between penis or scrotum size and your sexiness and ability to make love—or in fact any other form of activity! Your penis is only one small part of you, and your future wife will love your body no matter what size penis you end up having.

And despite the jokes, there is also no relationship between penis size and a man's height, weight or shoe size!

(ii) Pubic hair

There are also five stages of pubic hair growth in boys. Again, check these out to see where your own development is currently at. There's also diagrams on page 46

Stage 1: Childhood. There is no real pubic hair on your genitals. You may have a light fluff of hair not unlike the hair on your body or arms.

Stage 2: First pubic hairs. Pubic hair growth generally starts around the base of the penis, but you'll need to look closely to identify it! This could start anytime between age nine and 13 years. The hair is rougher and usually darker than the body hair; it may be a little curly. This stage of hair growth may or may not match what's happening in your penis and scrotum.

Stage 3: The hair gets thicker, darker in colour and for some boys curly. There is more hair and it could extend to the scrotum. Again this stage may or may not be in keeping with the changes in your penis and scrotum.

Stage 4: The hair at this stage pretty much looks and feels as it will do as an adult. However it still is limited to the pubic area, usually forming a triangle between the thighs.

Stage 5: The hair now is coarse and thick. It feels different to the hair elsewhere in your body. In most boys it now extends to the thighs and up as a peak towards the umbilicus (belly button). What you have now is your adult pattern. Again, what is happening with your pubic hair growth may be different from the rate at which your penis and scrotum are developing.

Stage 1

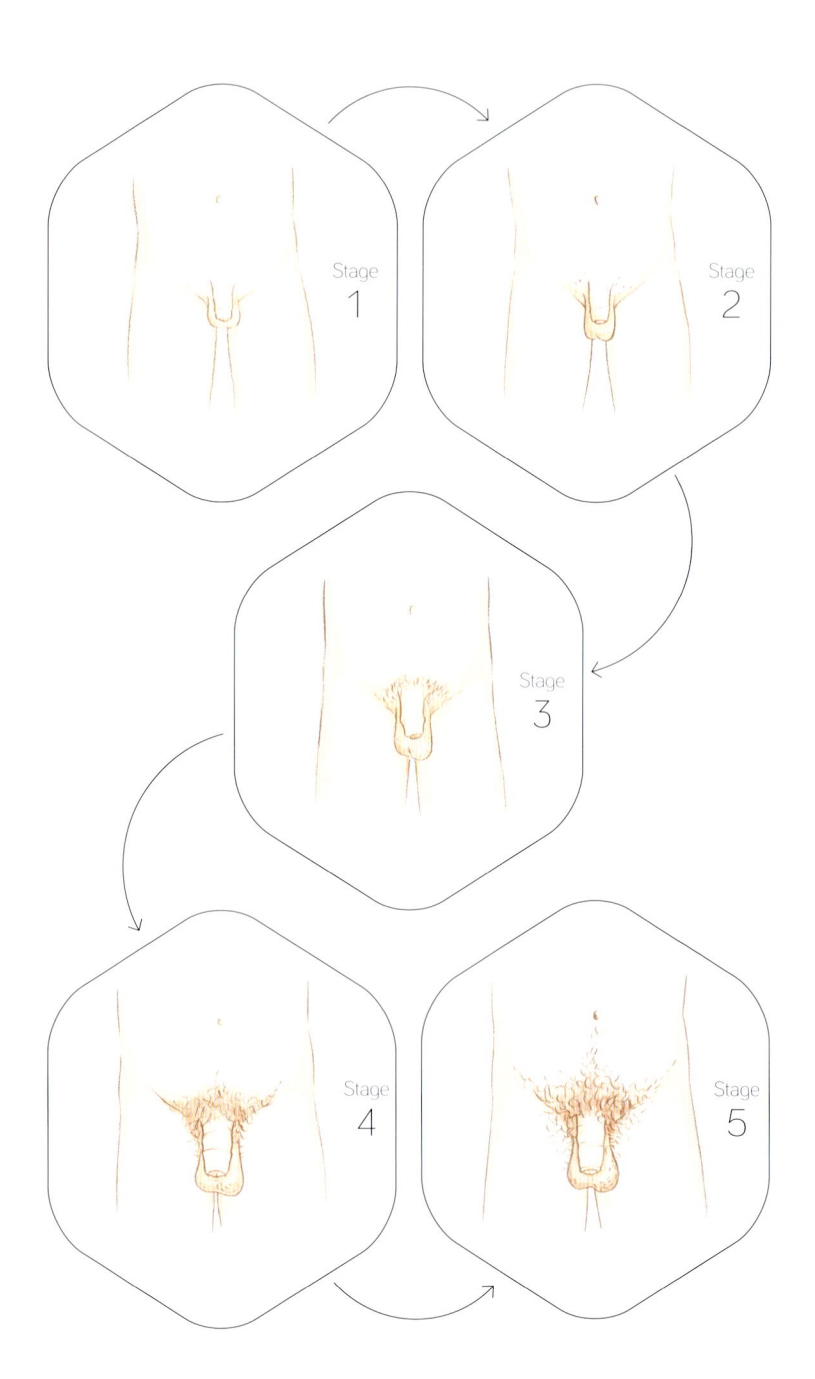

Stage 2

Stage 3

Stage 4

Stage 5

⚠️ Alert

Ethnicity

As well as individual differences, what your pubic hair feels like (the texture) and how it grows depends on your family genes and on your ethnicity—where your parents and their families came from. For some people with Asian heritage, adult pubic hair development does not go beyond Stage 3 or 4. The hair would also be finer and sometimes straight rather than curly. This difference in the texture of pubic hair can be seen in girls as well.

Now that you've worked out what external genital and pubic hair stage you are at, put the paper away. You can come back to it in six months and see how much you have changed.

Take-away message: You are lovely—just the way you are

Every one of you is different. You're at varying stages of body and genital development—even if you are the same age. Some are small, others larger; some more hairy, others less. The point we want to make here is that you are perfect and precious just as you are.

Remember what the Apostle Paul tells us: 'Do you not know that your bodies are members of Christ himself?' (1 Corinthians 6:15a); and again later in the chapter, 'Do you not know that your bodies are temples of the Holy Spirit, who is in you, whom you have received from God? You are not your own; you were bought at a price. Therefore honour God with your bodies' (1 Corinthians 6:19–20).

Your bodies are special not because of what they look like, but because they were created by and for Jesus Christ. That is why you are to use your body to glorify God.

But how do you do that?

Firstly, accept your body for what it is and don't waste time worrying about any part of it being too small or too big (or whatever). Look at your friends in the same way, loving them for who they are rather than what they look like or wear.

Whatever you do, don't laugh or put down others who are different in any way. This is cruel. It's not the way God wants his children to behave (Romans 15:2; Philippians 2:4).

Then use your body in ways that are appropriate and fun for your age; be involved in sport, music, walking, swimming and other healthy activities.

And avoid putting things into your body that pollute it. Keep away from drugs and alcohol, which will poison you, and from pornography and violent video games, which will trash your brain. We'll discuss how these negative things can affect you in the next chapter of this book.

⚠️ Alert

Good touch—bad touch

It is good and healthy for your parents to hug and kiss you. It is also normal for you to hug and be hugged by your grandparents, brothers and sisters. In some cultures, aunties and uncles also kiss and cuddle children.

As you enter puberty, you may continue to be OK with this or you might start to feel uncomfortable with this sort of touching by your family. Explain how you feel to Mum or Dad.

There is another sort of touching that is definitely 'bad'. This is any kind of touching—especially on your genitals or breasts—which makes you feel squeamish or uncomfortable. Even if it's by a family member or family friend, do not ignore your feelings. Stop the person from touching you by saying 'no' and moving away. Then tell your mum, dad or another trusted adult about it. Remember, it's the person *doing* the touching that is wrong, not you!

Ask Mum & Dad

You have assessed your own body development. Now it's time to chat with your parents. Go ahead—ask them. Remember, they most likely gave you this book so they want to help you! And they have bodies that changed at puberty too!

1 | What did you feel when your body started to change? Who helped you through that time?

2 | Mum: What was it like when you first menstruated? Dad: How did you feel when you first started having erections and ejaculating?

3 | Were you different to your friends of the same age? How did that make you feel?

We have looked at the changes in the body in detail. You now know how different each person is. You also know that whatever may happen in your body, you can be happy and fulfilled in the knowledge that God loves you—just the way you are.

The way you think and feel about your changing body actually starts in your brain, which is also the control centre for your actions and behaviour.

Let's look at that next.

Your brain: a work in progress

We have explored how the sexual parts of the body (a girl's breasts, genitals, body shape and body hair, and a boy's penis, scrotum, muscles and body hair) develop at different rates. You know now that no two of you will be identical at any point as you grow up.

However, everyone's *brain* looks the same! The brain looks like a soft mass of mountains and valleys. Boys' brains are a little larger (not necessarily smarter), but that's all. The internal wiring however—that's something else! The connections in the brain (like lots of electrical wires for information to travel along) are similar but slightly different in each person. And at puberty, your brain wiring is undergoing huge changes.

Getting to know your brain

The brain is the master control centre of your body. Your brain pushes the go-button on the sex hormones that drive the way your body changes in puberty. The brain also controls your emotions and feelings as well as your thinking and decision-making. We will look at just two parts of your brain—those that change the most at your age and are responsible for how you feel and act sexually.

These are the:

1 | Limbic lobe and hypothalamus—the emotional and quick-response sexual parts of your brain

2 | Grey matter of the cerebral cortex—the thinking and control part of your brain.

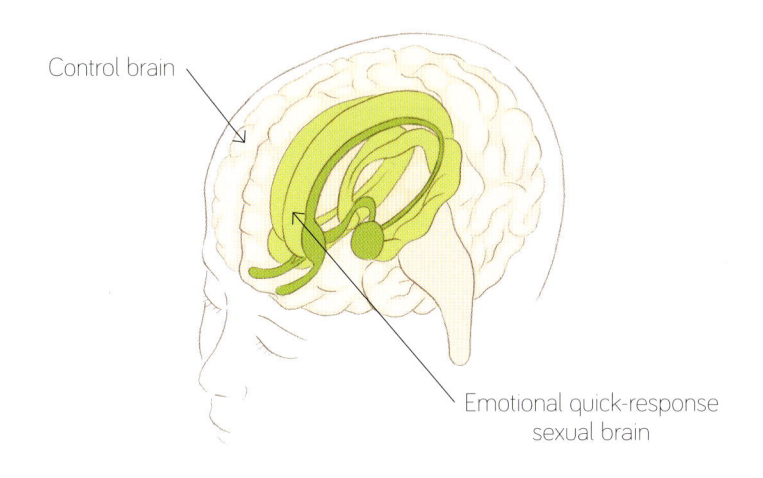

Control brain

Emotional quick-response sexual brain

The volcano: your emotional and sexual brain

Your emotional, sexual brain is quiet until puberty. Woken up by the increase in sex hormones (oestrogen in girls and testosterone in boys), your emotional and sexual brain then erupts in a rush of feelings and desires for quick rewards. It is truly like a volcanic eruption—sudden and dramatic.

When does this happen?

Just like your external body changes, it happens early in some people and later in others. Some boys and girls start thinking sexual thoughts at nine or ten years of age. On the other hand it's quite normal to feel comfortable in your 'child brain' well into your teens. So don't worry if you start having these feelings early. And relax if you have never had a sexual thought!

Your brain in puberty

The hormones we talked about in the last chapter also affect your brain.

Think spot

Changes

Your parents probably set rules for your behaviour. How do you feel about those rules?

Have your feelings about rules your parents set changed recently? In what way?

Do you feel like you would like to try something new? Do something different? What is it?

Whose opinions really matter to you now? Mum and Dad's opinion? Your teachers'? Or your friends'? Why do you think that is?

Your developing emotional brain makes you want to try new and exciting stuff and do increasingly risky things. Even you yourself might look back at something you've done, and think 'Why did I do that? That was crazy!' The growth and rewiring of your quick-response brain make you want things that give you an immediate reward—a quick buzz. The erupting brain is impatient! 'Go on—do it now!' your brain commands.

You want to move away from parents' control towards your friends and peers. And you want to do it quickly. You see this as being 'independent' of the rules set by Mum and Dad.

You may feel like a superhero one moment and totally helpless the next. In some people these emotional changes happen so suddenly that it feels like an alien has taken over your brain and is dictating your thoughts and actions. This is because the control mechanisms of your brain are not developed. We will explore this later.

Then comes the most exciting (and sometimes frightening) thing: the awakening of sexual feelings. You feel attracted to girls or boys; maybe you're even attracted to someone of the same sex and wondering if you are 'gay' (**HOMOSEXUAL**). You may feel as though no-one else feels the way you do, no-one understands.

Relax.

All these feelings are an important part of growing up. They allow you to explore what it means to be an adult. Your brain is moving you from dependence (on your parents) to independence. You want to be free to make your own choices and decisions. And your brain says, 'I want it now!' In time these feelings will help you move away from your parents and develop your own identity as an independent person.

Alert

Brain changes

Sometimes the rate at which these feelings develop can be confusing and even frightening. If you feel upset or scared, talk to your parents, your youth worker at church, or a school counsellor. Don't try to deal with the feelings by yourself.

What does it mean to be free?

Christians can be sure of one thing: true freedom does not come from throwing off the rules and controls of your parents and teachers and following what your friends and peers are doing. To blindly follow what friends, media and the internet tell you is not freedom—it's being a slave to the world!

True freedom comes from knowing that God loves you, and then following what he wants for your life. To live God's way, you need to learn how to control the roller-coaster of emotions and sexual feelings in your brain.

The Bible tells us that self-control is a fruit of the Holy Spirit (Galatians 5:22–25). It will empower you to say 'no' when you feel like doing something stupid and dangerous. It will motivate you to walk away from something which you know is dangerous and unhealthy, even when it feels good at the time or gives you a temporary buzz.

Self-control is a 'fruit' that starts out small and develops into something good and healthy. And like all fruit, it is something that must be carefully looked after. The ability to make wise choices is a skill that you need to practise and develop with the help of more mature people.

Let's look at the part of your brain that is involved in self-control: the thinking and control part.

The wet blanket: your slow-developing control brain

Your brain is about 95% of its adult size by age six. But the grey matter, or thinking and control area of the brain, continues to get thicker as you grow. The brain cells make extra connections; much like a tree grows extra branches, twigs and roots. In the front part of the brain (called the prefrontal cortex)—the area involved in making decisions, judgement, organisation, and planning—the thickening of this grey matter is fastest at about age 11 in girls and age 12 in boys, roughly about the same time as puberty.³

And this front part of the brain (the control centre—the part that tells you 'yes, go for it', or 'no, hang on, that's crazy!'—will continue to grow and mature until you are over 20 years old. It is a work in progress.

Do you sometimes find yourself confused as to what to do or say? Or worse, saying something and then thinking 'Where did that come from?' Have you agreed to do a crazy, risky activity without working out why it may be dangerous? You love someone one moment and want to run away the next? Sometimes you feel so low and confused that you want to escape everything—maybe even hurt yourself?

Blame it on your still-growing control brain—your immature prefrontal control mechanism! Now there's a great excuse for the next time your mother yells at you for doing something crazy at home. Try saying something like 'Mum, it's the fault of my underdeveloped control cortex!'

Do you see why we call it the 'wet blanket'? It's like something wet smothering the flames of your emotions and sexual urges as they erupt—and it's probably not doing a very good job!

So, what does this mean?

Simple: it means that you need help in making decisions. We don't mean that you can't make up your own mind about the type of cereal you have for breakfast. We are talking about the big decisions. There will be times when your emotional quick-response sexual brain will take you hurtling towards a cliff. And your immature control brain won't be in a position to make the decisions needed to stop it in time. You won't

---

3. *Frontline* 2002, Interview: Dr Jay Giedd, viewed June 25 2014, <http://www.pbs.org/wgbh/pages/frontline/shows/teenbrain/interviews/giedd.html>.

see the dangers, but adults who love you (with their mature prefrontal lobe and years of life experience) will know the risks and consequences.

Before you do something that may change your life—like sending that silly sexy text, getting sexually active, joining your friends in bullying someone or buying those sexy clothes—*stop. Ask for advice. Listen*. It may not seem so cool at the time but it may save you heaps of trouble later.

It may even save your life.

The writer of Proverbs (1:8–9) understood this. He advises young people to listen to their parents' teaching. He says that this advice will be symbols of honour, guidance and protection to you as you go through life.

Ask Mum & Dad

It may seem to you that your parents just don't understand how hard it is for you not to join in with your friends. But think for a moment: your parents were young too. So talk to them. Ask them:

1 | What were some of the things that you were really confused about at my age?

2 | Who helped you to decide what to do?

3 | Did you take their advice? What happened?

Let's talk a little more about the control mechanism of your brain.

Remember we said that at this stage of your brain development the brain wiring is undergoing huge changes. These changes are a little like pruning a plant. The branches (called axonal connections) that are used are kept and strengthened and the ones that are neglected and unused are removed. Your brain works on a 'use it or lose it' principle.

So, what nerve pathways are you building?

What are you doing, watching, reading and even thinking? These are the connections that will be hardwired into your brain for use later. This is serious stuff! What you feed your brain now will stay with you into teenage and later.

Is it any wonder that the Apostle Paul said, 'whatever is true, whatever is noble, whatever is right, whatever is pure, whatever is lovely, whatever is admirable—if anything is excellent or praiseworthy—think about such things' (Philippians 4:8).

What are you feeding your brain?

Let's find out! Here's an activity to help you think more about this.

Working out your Philippians score

Starting Friday afternoon, write down a list of what you and your friends do over a weekend.

At the end of the weekend, go back and look at what you have written. Give each entry a score of 0 to 8, where '8' fits into all standards of Philippians 4:8 (true, noble, right, pure, lovely, admirable, excellent and worthy of praise) and '0' is an activity that does not fit into any of these.

What is your total 'Philippians' score? What thoughts and actions could you change to increase your score?

Alert

Zero score activities

Alcohol and recreational drugs affect your brain development. In the short term, they remove what little control you have of your actions and lead you to do crazy things that you will regret. In the longer term, the use of alcohol and drugs affect the actual wiring of your brain, leading to poor performance at school, incompetence in other activities, and poor social skills.

Pornography: Photos, internet sites, video games or music clips that have sexual images which lead you to have sexual feelings are all **PORNOGRAPHY** (or 'porn'). Looking at these will rewire the brain circuits as we said above. Regular use will take you to dark places where you will question your body, your identity and your very self-worth, and do very stupid, self-destructive things—things that will come back to haunt you when you are older and want to develop a romantic relationship with a man or woman.

Violent video games: Many video games available today have unnaturally high levels of violence. They train your brain circuits to accept violence as a normal part of life. Feeding your brain on these will lead your brain to think that the way to get what you want in life—to be a winner—is to use violence. This is unhealthy. Above all it is not worthy behaviour for you, a child of God (James 1:19–20).

We have looked at God's word on sex. We then checked out the changes in your body as you grow up, and the meaning of the rewiring and growth that's taking place in your brain.

All this may seem a little 'whatever' to you. OK, so you know that your body grows at a different rate to your best friend. And you now understand that your brain is a work in progress and that, as a result, you need to work on your self-control and watch what you feed your brain, even though that may be easier said than done.

What you probably want to know now is, 'What does this really mean for me today?' This is what we will discuss in the next chapter.

Knowing who and whose you are

Your rapidly changing body and the emotional roller-coaster of your brain can lead to confusion.

When you look at yourself in the mirror, do you think 'Who is this person?'

Or when you are with your friends, do you think 'How can I be someone they will admire, love, or want to be like? How can I get them to think that I am cool/attractive/cute/awesome/sweet?'

Who the world wants you to be

Because you're struggling to understand who you are as a person, you're particularly vulnerable to the world's messages about what it means to 'be' someone. These days it seems normal to ignore God and Jesus, and to live life our own way. But God made the world and us, and so living our own way doesn't actually work—when we try, we end up destroying ourselves. The world's standards for success and importance don't actually result in peace and happiness, even though everyone pretends that they do.

In this section, we'll go through three worldly ways of thinking about your body and your sexuality, and show you how they end up making you miserable.

Then in the next section we'll show you how Jesus' way is good and healthy.

Being better or having more than others

The world says that to 'be' someone, you have to be better than other people in some way (looks and personality) or you have to have more of something than others (friends, money, Facebook likes, Twitter followers etc.).

But is this true?

Think spot

Your sense of self-worth

Look at yourself in the mirror. Imagine that there is someone there with you giving you advice on how you could be better and more popular. What would this person be telling you?

Try thinking of statements such as:

'You should be more ____' or 'less ___.'

'You are not _____ enough.'

'You would be happier if you had more____.'

'You are so bad at ____.'

'If you did more of ___ (or less of ___) you would be more popular.'

Maybe your inner style guru didn't have anything to say to your reflection other than: 'I like you; you're great just the way you are'. If so, congratulations! You have a really good view of your own body and self.

However there may be some of you who completed the questions by telling the reflected person things like 'You should be hotter, thinner, taller, stronger, or more tanned, less hairy or prettier'. You might have simply said, 'You should be more attractive!' or 'If you were more pretty/handsome you would have a boy/girlfriend'.

What you are doing is *comparing* your body and your looks (well, your reflection) to your friends or peers or maybe to a movie star, pop icon or magazine image.

What other things matter when you think about your self-worth and significance?

How about your *performance* at something? 'I would be happier if I was *better at* … the latest video game/sports/school etc.' Did you think you would like to be the funny guy or better at speaking to people? Or less shy when in a new group?

Or maybe it's about hanging out with the cool kids at school? Maybe your popularity with the pretty girls or good-looking guys?

What is the problem with basing your self-worth and identity on how you look or your success at something?

The problem is that there will *always* be someone who is thinner, prettier, more muscled, less hairy, and so on—someone who is *better* at anything you really want to do or be.

There will *always* be someone who is more popular with the pretty girls and hot guys, someone who is more confident than you, someone with more Facebook friends, more gadgets, whatever.

So what happens?

You end up sad that you don't live up to the standards you have set, or else you feel that you need to criticise or bully others who have less to make yourself feel better.

You need help to deal with these feelings.

Some young people don't have an adult to help them, or they don't feel able to ask for help. They try to deal with the sadness and frustration on their own by pushing it inside and hiding their true emotions. This is dangerous. These feelings can get worse and even lead to **DEPRESSION**. And doctors like myself see the results. Almost half of all teenage girls and about one in five boys say they are unhappy with their body. School counsellors and doctors tell us that they are seeing more and more girls and boys your age who cut themselves, or harm themselves in some other way, trying to cover their sadness and depression with the physical pain.

Ask Mum & Dad

When you were growing up, what was important to you about how you looked and behaved? Did you feel confident about yourself? Or did you feel sad or self-conscious about your body?

Who helped you work through these issues?

Did the way you pictured yourself change as you got older?

⚠ Alert

Getting help

If reading this makes you feel sad or depressed in any way, or you have a friend who is struggling with these feelings, talk to someone. Tell Mum or Dad, or if it's easier, talk to your teacher, a counsellor or an older person at church.

If you don't feel that you can talk to someone you know, call a help line with trained counsellors who are keen to listen and offer advice confidentially.

One such service is the Kids' Helpline at kidshelp.com.au or you can call them free of cost by dialling 1800 55 1800 (within Australia).

Some young people express their need to be better or have more than others by behaving badly. They may say things to put down or humiliate others—by bullying them—and this in turn makes them feel better about themselves. If this happens to you, try to remember that this is *their* problem, not yours!

⚠ Alert

Bullying

Have you been the target of bullying or any form of harassment? It may have been something someone said or a physical attack. It may have been a nasty or threatening text message or photo sent by phone, in an email or posted on the net.

> Or maybe this has happened to a friend or schoolmate.
>
> You do not have to put up with bullying. Talk to Mum and Dad and report it to your teacher or coach.

Your 'selfie' identity

The Oxford Dictionary word of the year for 2013 was 'selfie'. The popularity of selfies says that boys and girls today value how they look and, more importantly, how other people see them. This is so important to them that they 'must' post regular photos or videos of their faces and bodies on Instagram, Facebook and other social media sites. Sometimes they pull faces and frown for an 'ugly selfie'. But more often, they display their bodies in explicit (sexual or suggestive) poses or expose their breasts or genitals. Today some older teenagers even post pictures of themselves immediately after sexual activity in what is called 'post-sex selfies'.

Taken just a small step further, some young people start to believe that they actually are the person that their internet profile, selfie or avatar shows them to be! Their profile says to the world, 'Look at my outrageously fun life! My perfect face! My beautiful body! I'm here! I'm important! I matter! I am the best!'

The problem is: you'll never be *the* best, online or in real life. There will always be someone who is more attractive or more popular than you.

Plus, you're putting yourself under pressure to be even more sexy or raunchy in the next photo. Do you really want to do that? To show more and more of your body, in poses that are even more crazy and unnatural? Is that who you really want to be?

Think about it: you're putting your body out there for strangers to perve at and fantasise about.

Think spot

Self-check on personal behaviour

What does my Facebook profile, blog or webpage say about how I want people to see me? What do the photos I post on Instagram say about me as a person?

Who are my role models online? Who do I try to copy in the way I dress, act and talk?

Why do I do this?

Are you following your hero?

We follow people we admire. We want to be like them. It's obvious in young people; you might have heard people talking about (maybe complaining about!) 'youth culture' or 'youth idols'. But it's actually not limited to young people—everybody does it. We copy those people we admire: we wear the same style of clothes and hairstyles, perhaps even walk and talk like them. Sometimes this copying includes getting piercings or tattoos. Sadly, some young people starve themselves to get thin enough to look like their idol. Or they get drunk or take drugs to mimic a pop star or sports icon to appear 'tough' or rebellious.

Copying isn't always bad. In a moment, we're going to talk about how we're supposed to copy Jesus—to live like him; 'walk' and 'talk' like him. The question for now is: who's influencing you, especially your image or sexual behaviour? And are they pointing you towards—or away from—Jesus?

Think spot

Who do your friends and peers want to be like?

Who do your friends and peer group admire and mimic? Think about celebrities, models, TV personalities, singers or bands, and sportspeople.

What do your friends and peer group do to appear and act like these people? Think about their clothes and/or hairstyle; what they eat and drink; the music they listen to; how they aspire to look or act when they are old enough (perhaps they plan to get a tattoo or piercings, drink alcohol or try drugs).

What about you? Who do you admire? Whose opinions matter to you?

Think spot

Important people in your life

List the most important people in your life. (Choose at least five.) These are the people whose opinions matter to you most.

What do you do to please them, so that they like you?

Are they your role models? Would you try to copy them in the way you dress, act and talk?

You will copy people you admire and will want to act in ways that please people who matter to you. This is why you need to choose your friends and role models carefully.

Ask Mum & Dad

Who were the people they wanted to be like at your age?

How did that make them behave?

Ask if they have photos!

Who Jesus says you are

As Christians, the most important question isn't who you are, but *whose you are*: who do you belong to—Jesus or the world? If we belong to Jesus, he'll show us how to live in a way that's good and healthy.

Belonging to Jesus

The good news is: if we belong to Jesus, we don't have to compare ourselves or do anything to be like anyone else. You are special because you are God's child—his beloved son or daughter—and you are a part of his forever family, the Church. It doesn't matter what you look like, how skinny, fat, tall or attractive you are. Even your popularity doesn't matter. You can be talkative or shy, outgoing or introverted. You are one of a kind and special to God as his child.

God made you (Genesis 1, 2). And he sent his one and only Son, Jesus, to die on the cross for you, and rise from the dead, so that you could have a special place with him in heaven forever (Ephesians 1:11–14). When we trust in Jesus, God gives us his Holy Spirit to live inside us, to teach us the truth from the Bible, and to guide us through all the ups and downs of life. He loves you that much!

As a part of God's family, you're a brother or sister to Jesus! You can call the creator of the universe 'Dad' (Galatians 4:6)! In Romans 8:15, the Apostle Paul tells us:

> *The Spirit you received does not make you slaves, so that you live in fear again; rather, the Spirit you receive brought about your adoption to sonship. And by him we cry, 'Abba, Father'.*

You don't have to follow some crazy lifestyle to be popular and liked. You have the ultimate 'like' from the creator of the universe: God.

This doesn't mean we can ignore everyone else around us, and be rude to them and say 'I don't care what you think about me. Jesus loves me, so you can get lost'. Being a child of God doesn't mean we ignore our earthly relationships. We're still a child of our parents, a brother or sister, a student, friend, and so on.

The challenge for us now is to live all these other relationships *the way Jesus wants us to live*. If you're God's child, then Jesus is your brother. So admire him, and try to copy how he lived when he was here on earth. Read the Bible. See how he behaved, and how he treated others. Listen to his instructions, and what he taught his disciples, and then go and live the same way.

For example, many of you reading this will already feel secure and confident knowing that God loves you, that your parents and family love you, as does your church. You'll already have a healthy attitude to your body and your sexuality. That's great.

This puts you in a good position to help other young people—Christian or not—who are struggling. You could listen to them and let them share their struggles and fears with you. Then encourage them to get some help from a reliable adult, a school counsellor or a church leader you both trust.

This is going to be inconvenient. It'll take time and energy. It may not be easy or fun.

But think about it—this is what Jesus did, isn't it? He has the perfect self-identity: he's the Son of God! But he came down to earth so that we could be forgiven and made new again. He pointed us to the ultimate counsellor: God himself!

Ask Mum & Dad

All this talk of changing how you live may be confusing to some of you.

Take time to talk to Mum and Dad about the challenges they faced when growing up.

How did their values and the way they lived as Christians clash with what their non-Christian friends did and said?

How did they cope?

Share with them any problems you have in living as a member of God's family within your circle of friends and peers.

Take time to pray together as a family for God's help as you live as Jesus wants you to.

Think spot

Helping others

Think of your friends at school, church or in your sporting team.

Are any of them going through any of the 'alerts' in this book?

Who can you take them to for help?

Alert

Don't get out of your depth!

Do *not* try and help your friends all on your own! Problems with self-esteem and behaviour are often a lot more complicated than someone your age can handle or solve. Schools have professional counsellors to deal with this sort of thing. Church leaders know how to respond, and can also call on professional help. You want to help your friend—excellent! The best help you can give them is to go with them to a reliable adult who has experience and training.

Belonging to God's family

When we belong to Jesus, we belong to the rest of his people too—the Church. We are influenced by the people in our local church and youth group (the ministers, youth leaders, and our church 'uncles' and 'aunties').

And, believe it or not, the way we act and talk also influences others.

So let's talk about how to be a positive influence on each other. How can we help other young people to think and act in a godly way, especially as we go through all the ups and downs of sexual development?

Boys are generally turned on by anything that is even remotely sexual. So, girls: if the clothes you're wearing emphasise or expose your breasts, thighs and/or bottom, you're being seductive (sexually tempting), whether you mean to or not. Boys: the way you dress and act can also be a turn-on for your Christian sisters, so take care what you wear too. When you're around girls, don't stare at their bodies or flaunt yours. And definitely don't fantasise about the girls.

This *does not mean* that we should be ashamed of our bodies. Beauty is good. In Psalm 45, the psalmist says the king of Israel is 'excellent' (Psalm 45:2); the Hebrew word is literally 'beautiful'. And the king's bride is beautiful too (Psalm 45:11). So don't be ashamed of your body, but save it for your marriage partner to enjoy (1 Peter 3:3-4; 1 Timothy 5:1–2).

This *does mean* we shouldn't display our bodies as if we were some product for sale in a shop. When you walk into a shop, you'll see big signs saying 'For sale! Going cheap! Lowest price ever!' Is that really what you want to say about your own body?

Your body is good. Your body is beautiful. Jesus loves your body, and so do your parents, family and real friends—just as you are. Choose clothes that make you feel good about yourself, but that are also modest and tasteful.

Think spot

Public profiles

Have a look through your friends' Facebook profiles or Instagram photos, or their blog or Weebly websites. What messages do their photos and posts send?

Who are some of the popular music celebrities today? Check their websites. What do their pages say about them?

What are these 'profiles' aiming to do?

Do they 'build up' those who view them? Listen to their music and the lyrics (words)—are these good for someone your age to be singing or listening to?

Ask Mum & Dad

Having done the Think spot above, discuss your thoughts on your friends' profile pictures and the music icon webpages with Mum and Dad.

You've thought about and discussed how your friends present themselves to the world. What about you?

Think spot

Dressing to impress?

What clothes make you feel good about yourself?

Are they also clothes that are modest and tasteful? If not, why do you think that is?

How can you bring these two together?

Ask Mum & Dad

Discuss the Think spot above with Mum and Dad. What do they think makes you look attractive while being respectable and modest?

Your peer group as part of God's family

Let's make our churches and youth groups the kinds of places where people are respected for how they act, not how they look. This doesn't mean that we mock people who are outwardly attractive. As Christians, our actions and speech should say, 'looks don't matter here—your character does'. Let's encourage people to grow in the fruit of the Spirit (Galatians 5:22–23) showing kindness, faithfulness and patience. Never mind people's outer beauty; build up their inner beauty.

Think spot

Talking about each other

What kind of language do you use when talking about the people in your youth group? Do you say they're 'hot', 'cute' or 'sexy'? Or 'kind', 'generous' and 'patient'?

Why do you describe people the way that you do?

What does it say about the way you view them?

So here we have it. You are special because you are a child of God and you belong to Jesus' family. And once you know that, you can live bravely as Jesus wants you to—loving other people the way he has loved you.

How good is that?!

Conclusion

Where have we been?

Let's wrap things up.

God loves sex: he made it. Sex is not 'bad' or 'dirty'; it's very, very good. Because it's so good, we need to use it in the special context where it belongs: marriage.

God made us so that the sexual parts of our bodies develop in certain ways and at certain times. We may not always understand what's happening to us. That's OK; God does—he's in control.

Also, the way our brain develops makes us want to try new things. That's great. But it means we need to listen to older, more mature people if they warn us that we're about to do something stupid that we'll regret later.

God has given us loving, caring parents, and more experienced people to guide us as we go through this stage of life. (That's why I wrote this book!)

Jesus loves us just the way we are. If we trust Jesus, then he makes us one of God's children, part of God's family. So we don't have to prove ourselves to anyone. We can be happy in God's love. And we can try and care for others like Jesus cares for us.

Where are we now?

Think spot

A time for self-reflection

How do *you* feel about what you have learned in this part of the book?

What sections were new to you?

Did any sections make you feel happy? Sad? Challenged to do something?

Talk to Mum and Dad about how you feel.

Live confidently for Jesus—even if people don't appreciate you

Most of you will be comfortable with what you have read. That's great! Get out there among your friends and peers. Be out and proud for Jesus.

One warning, though. If we live for Jesus, we won't always be popular. Jesus said:

> Remember what I told you: 'A servant is not greater than his master.' If they persecuted me, they will persecute you

also. If they obeyed my teaching, they will obey yours also. (John 15:20)

Jesus loved people, healed the sick, fed the hungry, and protected the weak. What reward did he get for it? He was nailed to a cross to die an agonising death. In the same way, when we try to live for Jesus and care for people, they won't always appreciate it. Sometimes, they may even hate us for doing the right thing.

Don't get mad or try to get even; do what Jesus said—'Love your enemies and pray for those who persecute you' (Matthew 5:44).

But don't just bottle up the pain inside of you. If you get paid out for doing the right thing, talk to someone about it—your parents, a teacher, a church leader, or another reliable adult. They will help you to deal with your feelings. They may even be able to do something about it.

Seek help if you need it

If you're feeling bad about anything you've read—sad, guilty, anxious, or just confused—you need to talk to someone. The best people to answer these questions are your parents. However, some of you may not have a mum or dad, or you may not feel comfortable talking to them. If so, find another adult you trust: an aunty, uncle, youth worker or school counsellor.

If you don't have anyone you can talk to, you can contact the Kids' Helpline at kidshelp.com.au or you can call them free of cost by dialling 1800 55 1800 (within Australia) or email them via the website.

You can start by saying 'I am feeling _____. Is this normal?' or 'Can we please talk about some things that are bothering me?'

Do this before moving on to Part 2 of this book.

Where are we going?

Part 2 of the book is an A–Z of topics and questions girls and boys your age have asked us. It will build on the information you've already received. We pray that this knowledge will empower you to enjoy life as you grow from a child to an adult, and to be more confident as you face the challenges along the way.

PART 2

Introduction

In this section of the book you will find information on specific topics on growing up, sex and behaviour. These are listed in alphabetical order. The topics we discuss are drawn from questions that young people your age have asked in the many years that I have been speaking and teaching about sexual health. There are also some definitions from Part 1 that need further explanation.

There are some things you need to keep in mind when reading this section of the book:

1 | Use it to find out information on a particular issue or topic. Don't try reading it from A to Z; that would be information overload and you won't gain as much.

2 | As in Part 1, we start many of the topics with a **Think spot**. Feel free to make notes on how you feel about the topic or any questions you may still have.

3 | Some of you may find the information too detailed for you to understand. Use the **Ask Mum and Dad** discussion sections to clear up any issues you have.

4 | Some of the topics may make you feel uncomfortable. This may be because your brain is still not grown up enough for them. Or else it may be because of something you have seen or experienced. Either way, talk to Mum, Dad, a teacher or youth worker about it. The person who gave you this book is the first person to go to.

5 | Many of the topics have a 'See also' note at the bottom to refer you to similar topics.

A–Z of topics

Abstinence

To 'abstain' is to choose to hold yourself back from doing something. The word abstinence is used when a person keeps from an activity they may like or want to do, like drinking alcohol or something sexual like having sexual intercourse.

Think spot

List some of the things you have 'abstained' from.

What has made you choose not to do those things?

Abstaining from something that your friends are doing, particularly when it looks like fun, is not easy. For example, you may think 'Why shouldn't I just give in and let my boyfriend touch between my legs? It feels nice'. Or 'Why can't I have a beer? All my friends are doing it'.

Firstly, when it comes to sex, the Bible is very clear. Sexual intimacy, whether it's allowing someone to touch your genitals or breasts or having sexual intercourse, is for marriage. In the creation story, we clearly see the order of events. A man will be 'united' with his wife and then they will have 'naked and no-shame' sex, and become one flesh (Genesis 2:24–25).

In the New Testament, acting against God's plan for sex (sexual immorality) is said to be similar to worshipping idols (Acts 15:20, 29; 21:25)—it's considered to be sinful in God's eyes.

Secondly, it is important that you understand that any behaviour, whether it is sexual or not, is a choice you make. You are not a ball of sex hormones, following every desire you feel. You are a child of God (Galatians 4:4–6; Ephesians 1:4–6), made in his image (Genesis 1:26). Jesus died so that you could be forgiven and live as God's friend, and he gives you the gift of self-control (Galatians 5:22–24).

Make wise choices. Don't follow what your peers, the media and music videos say you should do. We know that this is not always easy, so ask for help from your parents and other adults you admire. If you have Christian friends in your group, suggest that you encourage, help and pray for one another when the peer pressure gets too much. If you don't have Christian friends, we would suggest you find a youth group that meets at lunchtime at school or a youth group at your local church. This will give you a like-minded group of people to hang out with.

Ask Mum & Dad

What were the messages they heard from their friends, the media and magazines about sexual activity and intimacy when they were younger?

Was there someone who helped them to resist the message to get sexually active?

See also | **CELIBACY**

Anal sex

Anal sex means sexual activity involving the bottom. This is where the penis is inserted into the anus. It's sometimes referred to as 'rectal sex'. It was originally thought that this was an activity that was only practised by homosexual men. We now know that this is not the case. Some heterosexual (male/female) couples also have anal sex.

Anal sexual activity carries very real dangers. The anus was designed for the body's waste to be pushed out. It was not designed for objects to be inserted into, and the tearing of the delicate skin can lead to bleeding, infections and the transfer of sexually transmitted disease.

See also | **SEXUAL INTERCOURSE,
SEXUALLY TRANSMITTED INFECTIONS (DISEASES)**

Aphrodisiac

An aphrodisiac is any substance that is taken to increase a person's sexual desire. Some are made from plants; others are medications.

Alcohol and recreational drugs (like cocaine, marijuana, methamphetamines, 'Ice' and others) are used as aphrodisiacs by some women and men.

There is no evidence that any of these substances have any real effect in making a person sexier, or increasing sexual desire and arousal.

If you are ever offered anything suspicious by anyone (even a friend), say 'no thanks' and then tell Mum and Dad, a teacher or youth worker about it.

Alert

Do not ever accept or take anything suspicious you are offered or unsure of either at a party or in the playground.

1 | You do not need drugs and alcohol—your natural sexual urges (your emotional brain) will develop when the time is right for you. You can have lots of fun without being drunk or high.

2 | Alcohol and recreational drugs will make you lose what control you have in your maturing brain and you may end up doing something you later regret—like having sex or putting yourself in danger.

3 | Many of these so-called aphrodisiacs are habit-forming and you could get hooked on them (you won't be able to stop using them without the help of a doctor). This could destroy your developing brain and ultimately your life.

4 | You don't know what the illegal drugs are made from or mixed with. Most recreational drugs (other than alcohol and tobacco) are illegal and made by people who aren't experienced chemists or mix them with cheap ingredients such as drain cleaner to make more profit. As well as the effects of the drugs themselves, you could end up seriously ill or dead.

Body image

Your body image is how you see your own body and how you think others see you. It influences your self-esteem (the value you put on yourself) and how you dress and present yourself to others. We have discussed this in Part 1 of the book.

See also | Chapter 4

Brazilian wax and other pubic hair removal

A 'Brazilian' is the name given to the removal of all the pubic hair, either by shaving, waxing or laser treatment, usually for women (but also by some men). This is mainly done by waxing, where a hot or cold layer of wax is applied and then removed with adhesive strips. In laser hair removal, lasers and IPL (intense pulsed light) devices, (which are not technically lasers but work on a similar principle) are used by some women to reduce the amount of, or permanently remove, hair. Melanin (the colour) within the hair follicles is targeted, heating and damaging the hair follicles in an active growth cycle.

The popularity of this smooth, hairless look has been driven by fashion, movies and, unfortunately, pornography. Other than avoiding the embarrassment of bikini line hair poking out from a swimsuit, there is no reason for a young girl to wax, shave or laser her pubic area. When you are married, you can make these decisions to suit yourself and your husband.

Bullying

Think spot

Have you seen or heard someone being teased or laughed at for being different in some way? It may be because of the way their body looks (thin, fat, hair colour), their choice of clothes (not cool or trendy), their skin colour, nationality, assumed sexual behaviour, or a disability.

How did this make you feel? Did you do anything to help or stop this situation?

This kind of behaviour is bullying.

To bully someone is to harass, humiliate, embarrass, torment, threaten, pick on or intimidate them. It may be verbal (spoken) abuse such as name-calling, or a physical action such as pushing and shoving or violence. In your world of cyber communication it is more likely to be a nasty text message, email, Facebook post, an Instagram photo or a comment on a blog or webpage—this is called cyber bullying.

Ask Mum & Dad

What were their experiences of bullying when they were your age?

Discuss with them how bullying has changed because of the online world you live in.

Putting another person down is never OK—never! Not even if you think the person has done something wrong or deserves it.

Jesus is very clear in his teaching. We are called to love not just our fellow Christians (John 13:34–35). We are instructed to love our enemies (Matthew 5:44) and to pray for them. After all, Jesus forgave the people who abused him, to the extent of nailing him to the cross (Luke 23:34).

Alert

If you have been or are being bullied in any way, talk to Mum and Dad, or tell your teacher. Do not ignore it or think it will just go away.

If you see someone else being bullied, be a friend to them. If they are distressed, encourage them to report it to a teacher. Go with them if they are anxious.

See also | **CYBER BULLYING**, **CYBER COMMUNICATION**

Celibacy

The term celibate was originally used for someone who had decided—sometimes taken a vow or promise—to remain single and not marry. Today it is a word used for someone who makes the choice not to have any sexual relationship outside of marriage.

Some people stay celibate all their lives. It may be because they never get married, and remain as a single man or woman. Occasionally this choice is because they are attracted to people of their own sex (homosexual) and as a Christian, they make the decision not to act on these desires by having sexual intimacy with someone of their own sex.

It is possible to be celibate and very happy. We have explored in Part 1 how important relationships are. Most celibate single people have a rich friendship network. Whatever your friends or peer group may tell you, it is possible to live a full and happy life without sex.

See also | **ABSTINENCE**, **HOMOSEXUALITY**

Circumcision

The tip of the penis, called the glans, is very sensitive. It's covered by a fold of skin called the foreskin which is held down at the back by a band of tissue called the frenulum. This foreskin is cut off if the boy has the surgical procedure of circumcision.

If you have not had this procedure, it is important that you gently push back the foreskin and wash the glans of your penis regularly when you have a bath or shower. This will prevent urine, semen and sweat and exfoliated skin (called smegma) from building up under the fold of skin and causing irritation, even infection.

Whether you have a foreskin or not will not affect your ability to have and enjoy sex when you are married.

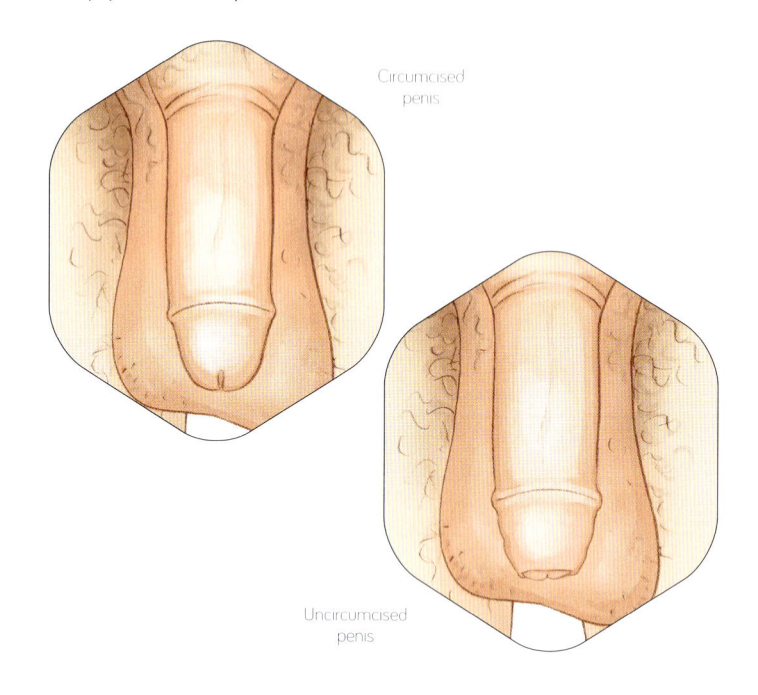

Circumcised penis

Uncircumcised penis

Circumcision goes back to the Old Testament, when God instructed Abraham to have all the Israelite boys and men circumcised (Genesis 17:9–11). This was part of what is called the 'covenant' (agreement) between God and the Israelites.

As Christians today, we don't *need* to be circumcised. People can see that we are Christians by the work God has done inside us, in bringing us to faith in Jesus Christ. This outward sign of circumcision is now unnecessary as we are recognised by our faith in Jesus Christ who died in our place (Colossians 2:11; 3:11).

Some parents decide for personal reasons to circumcise their sons. Others don't.

Ask Mum & Dad

If you are a boy, take a look at your penis. Are you circumcised?

Talk to your parents as to why they made the decision to either have you circumcised or not.

Contraception

The word 'conception' is used to explain the point at which pregnancy starts. So 'contraception' is anything that prevents a woman from getting pregnant. For a woman to get pregnant, her egg ('ovum' which is released about once a month from puberty to menopause) must meet and unite with a man's sperm (a process called fertilisation). This happens when a man and woman have sexual intercourse. In other words when a man puts his penis in the woman's vagina and deposits his sperms (semen) in the vagina (called ejaculation, cum, orgasm or many other everyday terms).

There are many types of contraception. Some (such as the contraceptive pill) prevent the egg (ovum) from being released in the woman. Others prevent the sperm and ovum from meeting. A condom, for example, is like a glove that fits over the man's erect penis and keeps the semen from escaping into the woman's vagina. A diaphragm is a dome-shaped device that a woman inserts into her vagina to prevent the sperm from entering her uterus (womb).

It is important for you to know that no contraceptive is 100% effective in preventing pregnancy and sexually transmitted infections.

You may learn more about contraception later in school. However, if you have any questions ask Mum and Dad.

⚠️ Alert

Some girls who have never had sexual intercourse get pregnant. How is that possible? It is because sperms are very good swimmers! So semen deposited even close to the vaginal opening, between the legs of the girls in the vulva region, can make their way into the vagina and up into the uterus. Pre-ejaculate (pre-cum) is a small amount of fluid (usually just a few drops) that's released from the penis before actual ejaculation. It's usually such a small amount that it can be hard to tell if any has come out, but it does have sperm in it.

The chance of getting pregnant from pre-cum is much less than the chance of getting pregnant from semen, but it is still possible.

The only really safe way to avoid a pregnancy is to abstain from sexual intimacy where there is contact between penis and vulva unless you are married.

Chromosomes

Chromosomes are what carry the genetic material from parents to children. Every cell in your body has these.

Each chromosome is made of a substance called deoxyribonucleic acid (DNA). Passed from parents to children, DNA contains the instructions that make you the unique person you are.

You have 23 pairs of chromosomes: one pair from Mum and one pair from Dad. This is why some of your physical and even emotional characteristics are like your mother and some like your father.

One pair of chromosomes is called the 'sex chromosomes'. These are what determine whether the baby develops testes and becomes a boy or ovaries and becomes a girl. A girl has two 'X' chromosomes; a boy has one 'X' and one 'Y' chromosome.

Cyber bullying

This is when a person is bullied and harassed using some form of electronic media. It may be in the form of a text message, email, Facebook post, Instagram photo or comment on a blog or website.

See also | **BULLYING, CYBER COMMUNICATION**

Cyber communication

What do you think life was like before smartphones—when a tablet was something your doctor prescribed when you were sick? And when, if you wanted to contact a friend, you sat down with pen and paper and wrote them a letter?

Ask Mum & Dad

How has communication between friends changed since they were your age?

How did they arrange to meet? Or send out party invitations?

It seems that we no longer need to open our mouth and talk. All our communication can be done on instant messaging and social media. We don't even need to move! Why meet in a café or talk on the phone when we can text? Yes, the virtual world of communication is replacing the face-to-face conversation … well, almost.

And we definitely do not need a pen and paper to express our feelings or moods. Happy, angry, annoyed … whatever—there's an emoticon for it!

What are the good things about cyber communication?

Apart from making it easy to keep in touch with friends via messaging, Skype and social media, the internet gives you the opportunity to get the latest information on anything and everything 24/7. You are the most informed and educated young people ever to have lived on this planet—all thanks to cyber communication.

Are there downsides to cyber communication?

We are created for relationships—relationships with *real* people. Your feelings are more open in the intimacy of a face-to-face chat. The person with you can see your expression and your body language, and hear your tone of voice. You are vulnerable. This is not so in cyber communication. In cyberspace, you can hide what you want, exaggerate the truth, and express opinions anonymously. Basically you can create a personality which may be very different from the person you really are. The scary thing is that most other people are also only presenting what they want the world to see. You could end up with a community (peer group, friends) who are all hiding behind a pretend identity.

We worship a God who became a human being for us. He lived with friends and enemies, before suffering and dying a humiliating death on the cross for us (John 1:14). In the flesh, intimate friendships with people who know and understand our doubts and personalities are important to us. It is much harder to experience this depth of feeling when you are in a cyber-relationship. Enjoy your cyber communication, but take time to nurture the real face-to-face meetings and fun times of friendship.

Another problem with cyber communication is the impulsiveness of it. You can type and send a message without much thought as to the possible effect it could have on the receiver or anyone else who might see or read it. Once it is on the internet, it is extremely difficult to take it back or delete its history.

Remember what we discussed about your brain in Part 1 of the book? Your emotional risk-taking brain is growing faster than your thinking control brain. You could very easily send a message or a photo that you later regret—sometimes as soon as you press 'send'.

Alert

Selfies, sexting and cyber bullying are all the result of this impulsive, emotional brain response.

Stop and think before you send your next text message or post something online. Is it really what you want to say or how you want others to see you? Remember that nothing is truly secret in cyber communication—a message or photo can be shown to lots of other people without your permission. How might your message or photo impact other people?

See also | **BULLYING**, **CYBER BULLYING**

Dating

Think spot

What do you think 'dating' means?

Are any of your friends currently dating?

How does this affect their behaviour and what they say about it?

Dating is basically any activity where two people share time together with the intention of getting to know each other better.

That seems quite healthy and normal, doesn't it? The problem is that at this point of your life, 'getting to know each other' often gets translated to mean sexual intimacy and activity between the boy and girl.

This is the danger in dating at a young age—sexual activity and ultimately intercourse is not always something you might plan or expect to happen until the heat of the moment. This is the time when your emotional brain totally overrules your thinking brain!

Ask Mum & Dad

What did dating involve when they were growing up? Was it even called 'dating'?

If your grandparents are available to talk to, ask them about how they met and got to know each other.

So, do you think that you are old enough to manage your feelings and actions?

Let's look again at what happens when you meet a boy or girl that you really like. Your emotional brain erupts in a rush of feelings: a longing to get to know this person better, to spend time with him or her, and perhaps be their special friend or boy/girlfriend. And yes, sexual feelings are a part of it. And you want this *now*. You don't want to wait; you can't wait! This is your emotional 'volcano' brain that's firmly in charge, rushing forward without your controlling 'wet blanket' brain to stop it. If all of this is sounding a little weird, you might like to go back and read the section on the brain (pages 51–57) in Part 1. The truth is that your emotional brain is pushing you towards the high-risk activity of one-to-one dating when your body and control brain is not ready for it.

So when will *you be ready to go out with a boy or girl in a dating relationship?*

There is no special age or developmental stage at which a girl or boy becomes ready to enter the dating scene. Rather, it is when you are mature enough to handle the intense emotions and decision-making pressures of a one-to-one relationship.

Dating is like walking through a minefield. To navigate your way through it safely, you need to be sure of three things which we call the three 'W's:

1 | Who you are.

You need to be very clear that your self-esteem and identity is based on who you are as a child of God and brother or sister of Jesus. We have discussed this in Part 1 (see pages 67–74).

You need to be certain that you are able to think and act independently of your boyfriend or girlfriend. That is, you can control how you behave sexually and are not worried about how popular you are or what your friends or others think of you. Your first priority is doing what God wants you to do. This needs a level of brain maturity and wisdom that you, as someone aged between ten and 14, are still developing.

When you see yourself as a child of God, you understand that other boys and girls around you are also children of God, and you treat them as members of your family. You will look at relationships, whether dating or friendships, differently. The question you should ask is not 'What can I or can't I do?' (or 'How far is too far?') but rather, 'How can I honour my brother or sister in Christ and build up our relationship in a God-honouring way?'

Does this sound different to what your friends say and do?

Ask Mum & Dad

In a world where your friends may say that any close friendship must automatically involve sex, having such a relationship without sexual intimacy may seem strange to you!

Ask Mum and Dad how the boys and girls in their day behaved towards each other as friends, without it being sexual.

If you have older brothers and sisters, talk to them too.

2 | What is happening in your body and brain?

You need to understand that your body and brain are especially fragile—it's like being on a swinging bridge between childhood and adulthood.

We discussed this in Part 1 of the book.

What you do with your body now matters. It will affect how your brain develops and the relationships you form with men and women later in life.

The Apostle Paul is very clear about this. In 1 Corinthians 6 he tells us that our bodies are part of Christ himself. He calls the body a 'temple' or home for the Holy Spirit. As Christians, we are called to use our bodies to honour God, not to use and abuse them for our selfish, sexual pleasures or give them to someone else to use. This, the Apostle tells us, is sexual immorality. And God hates that.

Don't put yourself in a position where your emotional, volcano-like brain may drive you to do something that your control brain hasn't had time to process and assess for risks.

3 | When to say 'no'.

Sometimes saying 'no' is the most difficult thing to do. It is about being strong enough to set boundaries in your friendships. You need to recognise the difference between making and keeping good friendships with both boys and girls (what is called non-sexual intimate relationships) and crossing the line to sexual teasing and flirting which can lead very quickly to sexual intimacy.

⚠ Alert

Girls: Keeping activity from progressing from something fun and friendly to sexual activity is particularly difficult when you are with an older and more experienced boy. If he is not a Christian and does not live by the godly principles of honouring and caring for women (1 Timothy 5:1–3), he may have greater expectations of what you, as a young Christian girl, may be prepared to do. Even though you might think that you are in control of the situation, listen to your parents' advice if they don't want you to be alone with a boy or to continue a relationship with him. Proverbs 1:8 advises us to listen to our father's instruction and not to forsake our mother's teaching. This is still great advice for today.

Ask Mum & Dad

Ask your mum and dad how to recognise the difference between friendly fun, teasing, flirting and harassment. This will help you to understand the difference between friendship and a relationship that is heading towards sexual activity or unwanted sexual attention. Talk about what you might do if your friendship with someone of the opposite sex is heading in the wrong direction.

Continue the conversation among your friends and in your youth group.

See also | Chapters 2 and 3

Depression

Everybody feels sad sometimes. None of us can be happy every waking moment of our lives. These temporary bouts of sadness are therefore normal.

Think spot

How do you deal with sad feelings?

Think of last week or the last two weeks. List all the times you felt sad.

What did you do during these times to deal with your feelings?

You may have dealt with the sad feelings by thinking happy thoughts or doing something that you enjoy. That sometimes works—but not always. On the other hand you may have talked to someone like your mum, dad, a teacher, or even someone who was involved in the incident that made you feel sad. Talking is the best way to deal with these sad feelings.

Depression is when you feel really sad for long periods of time (weeks, months or even years) and sometimes without any apparent reason. You may find that you no longer want to do things that you normally enjoy. You may feel very tired but not able to sleep, or you may want to sleep all the time.

Depression makes life more difficult to manage from day to day. It is more than just sadness—it's a serious illness.

If you feel that you are suffering from depression, talk to your mum and dad, a counsellor or teacher. You may just be going through a tough time, and talking about it may be all you need to do. On the other hand, they may take you to see your family doctor. Your doctor will then decide if you need counselling or medicine.

See also | **BODY IMAGE**

Erections and ejaculations

Think spot

What words have you heard used for the following:

1 | When the penis goes from being soft (flaccid) and hanging limp close to the body, to hard and standing at an upward angle away from the body (erect)?

2 | The moment when secretions (semen) come out of the tip of the penis?

The process by which the penis goes from being soft and flexible to hard, firm and larger is called an erection. The moment when semen comes out of the tip of the penis is called ejaculation.

You may have heard many words used for these (like getting a 'hard on', 'boner', or 'stiffy' for erection or 'cum' for ejaculation). Or else—especially if you are a girl—you may have never heard of these. Either way, it's OK. It is, however, best to use the correct terms for penis function as for any body part or function.

So, what is an erection and how does it happen?

The inside of the penis is made of a soft spongy tissue full of blood vessels. The urine tube (urethra) runs through the middle of it. Urine travels through the urethra when you go to the toilet and semen takes the same path when you ejaculate.

When the penis is in its soft state, there is an equal amount of blood coming in (arteries) and going out through the blood vessels (veins) in the penis. An erection happens when more blood is pumped into the penis than goes out. The spongy tissue in the penis fills with blood and the penis gets larger and harder. This is an erection.

Erections happen fast and often as you move through puberty. Sometimes they are in response to a sexual thought or feeling. Often they are called 'spontaneous erections': they happen unexpectedly and for no particular reason. This happens because the penis is very sensitive in the early teenage years (it has a lot of nerve endings and blood vessels) and because sex hormones go into overdrive. If and when this happens to you, relax. It's perfectly normal. It doesn't mean you're oversexed or something. And you don't have to masturbate or have sex to relieve the situation—these erections usually subside without an ejaculation. You're best just to ignore it when it happens. It can be embarrassing if you get an erection while you're in a public place, but try sitting down, placing something on your lap and distracting your thoughts.

⚠ Alert

If you have frequent or painful erections and this bothers you, talk to your mum or dad, or see your doctor. You are in a phase of growth and it's important to get this checked.

Ejaculation—the end point.

Whereas erections happen even in baby boys (a process we call reflex erections), ejaculations need sperm to be produced and mixed with other secretions from glands like the prostate to form semen. This happens after puberty, when your sex hormones kick in.

Ejaculation is the end point of sexual excitement in a man. It is the first external sign of sexual maturity and as such is a normal part of growing up.

Sometimes ejaculations happen in the night during sleep. This could be in response to a dream or just a muscle contraction associated with sleep. This is sometimes called a 'wet dream'. This is normal at puberty.

Ask Mum & Dad

Most boys move through the time of erections and first experiences of ejaculations without stress. Some, however, feel anxious about these changes and functions. This may happen if you think you are ahead of or behind your peer group in growing up sexually. If this is you, don't be embarrassed—please talk to Mum or Dad about it.

See also | **MASTURBATION, WET DREAMS**

Homosexuality

The term 'homosexuality' is used to indicate the sexual attraction that a person feels towards someone of the same sex. It is also called 'same-sex attraction' (SSA). This includes lesbian (girl-to-girl) and gay (boy-to-boy) sexual attraction.

Note: The term 'heterosexuality' is used to indicate that a person is sexually attracted to someone of the opposite sex—girl-to-boy and vice versa.

⚠ Alert

The terms 'homosexual', 'lesbian' and 'gay' are words that describe a relationship. They are not words to be used to tease or put another person down.

Just because a boy doesn't like to do what other boys consider normal (rough-and-tumble games, footy … whatever) doesn't mean that he is gay. The same applies to girls; there's nothing wrong with a girl who prefers sports and jeans to ballet and dresses.

If this sort of teasing and bullying happens to you, or you see it happen to someone else, bring it to the notice of a teacher, coach or your parents.

A few more things about homosexuality:

Just because a person feels sexually attracted to another does not mean that they have to be sexually intimate with that person. This applies whether you are homosexual or heterosexual.

The Bible is very clear about sexual activity. We see in the creation story how God created male and female (Genesis 1:27) and set up the pattern of sex within the marriage relationship of male and female (Genesis 2:24–25). Also, the Bible doesn't talk about homosexual (SSA) people; it only talks about homosexual acts (Romans 1:26–27). And these, the Bible says, are wrong (1 Timothy 1:9–11).

Self-control is a gift of the Holy Spirit (Galatians 5:22–25). Everyone—both heterosexuals and those with same-sex attraction—needs to practise self-control in all parts of our lives, including our sex lives.

It is estimated that there are 2–4% of people who feel same-sex attraction, and even more who feel attraction to both sexes (sometimes called bisexuals). If you feel this way, please talk to someone—Mum or Dad would be best. If this is too difficult, speak to a teacher, school counsellor or your youth worker at church. It may turn out that you are worrying unnecessarily. Or it may be that you are truly SSA. Either way, they will help you deal with the emotions and work out that the same-sex attraction is different to choosing to be sexually active.

Same-sex friendships are an important part of life. Loving someone of your own sex does not make you a homosexual. The best example we have is the friendship between David and Jonathan in the Bible (1 Samuel 20:17). Out of curiosity, you may have looked at or touched another person of your own sex. This does not make you a homosexual.

Your identity is not based on your sexuality, or anything else about your body or behaviour. Your true identity rests in being a child of God, redeemed by the death of Jesus (see Part 1, Chapter 4).

Ask Mum & Dad

What did they learn about homosexuality when they were growing up? Did they know anyone who was homosexual? Other than their sexual preferences, were these people different in some way to heterosexuals?

Hymen

Funny word, right? The hymen is a thin, fleshy tissue that stretches across part of the opening of the vagina. It does not completely cover the opening or else it would prevent menstrual fluid coming out.

The hymen can be stretched open the first time a girl has vaginal sex, which might cause some pain or bleeding. And despite what you may have heard, the hymen cannot grow back once it's been stretched open.

Some people, and some cultures, believe that a woman whose hymen has been stretched open is no longer a virgin. But having an intact hymen and being a virgin are not the same thing.

There are other ways that a hymen can be stretched open—by inserting something into the vagina (like a tampon or a finger), riding a bicycle, or doing sports. And some girls are born with so little hymen tissue that it seems like it was never there.

See also | **VIRGINITY**

Intersex

Sometimes things go wrong in how the genitals are formed when the baby is in the mother's womb. So instead of having a perfectly formed little penis and scrotum, or a vulva and vagina, a newborn baby may have partially formed (or what is called 'ambiguous'—neither one nor the other kind of) genitalia. This is called 'intersex'.

This condition is rare. For every 3000 to 4000 babies born, one will have some form of ambiguous genitalia.

The Bible tells us that we are created male and female. Our genitalia are an important part of this maleness and femaleness. How then should we understand people who are intersex?

Most times it is possible to determine whether the baby is a boy or girl depending on whether the baby has XY chromosomes (testes and testosterone—boy) or XX chromosomes (ovaries and oestrogen—girl). Sometimes this is more difficult.

Intimacy

Intimacy is being close to another person emotionally. It may or may not include physical closeness, but it always involves trust, the ability to tell the truth and know that you will be understood, loved and cared for—no matter what.

True friendship is intimate, as is the relationship between parents and children, or that between brothers and sisters.

Sexual activity in marriage is the most intimate physical thing two people can do. This is why the Bible calls it a 'one flesh' act (Genesis 2:24–25). But even married people have many other things they do together that demonstrate intimacy.

Ask Mum & Dad

What sort of non-sexual things do they do together that make them feel close and loving?

Love

🗨 Think spot

Can you remember the very first time you said 'I love ...'? What did you say that you loved?

As you got older, did the things you 'loved' change?

What would you say you love now?

You've been in love with someone or something all your life ... a teddy bear, Mum, ice-cream, the Wiggles®, whatever. Now maybe it's a celebrity or sports star. Maybe you love your best friend. Or maybe you even have a crush on someone? (See pages 16–18 of Part 1.)

The Bible has a lot to say about love. In Matthew 22:34–40 Jesus says that all the commands in the Bible stem from love: loving God and loving others. The Apostle John said 'God *is* love' (1 John 4:8).

At puberty, the fleeting feelings of sexual attraction you might feel towards a boy or a girl are the result of chemical changes in your brain that are getting you ready for the big event: the love for the person you will marry. So if you are a boy, enjoy the little thrills of attraction you feel towards that cute girl. Talk to her, be a friend, even a brother in Christ. The Apostle Paul wrote to the young man Timothy and told him to treat younger women as sisters, with absolute purity (1 Timothy 5:1–3).

Similarly, if you are a girl, make friends with boys, talk and learn to interact with them. Enjoy their company, but don't flirt and tease. (This includes doing things like blowing kisses or smiling and winking, sitting on their lap, cuddling, or pressing your body in close when you hug.)

⚠️ Alert

You never have to prove that you love someone by having sex with them. Anyone who says 'if you really loved me then you would ...' only wants to use you. The person (be it a boy or a girl) does not care for or honour you. If they threaten you or insult you because you don't want to do as they ask, they are not truly your friend or someone you want to be in relationship with. This is bullying at best and abuse at worst. Talk to Mum or Dad or report it to a teacher.

Translating love to sexual activity is called lust. At the core of lust is selfishness, disrespect and a lack of self-control—none of which are valuable characteristics in God's eyes. Talk to your mum or dad if you find yourself in a relationship where this happens.

When you are older, you may meet and fall in love with someone you want to marry. Then, the loving attitude of your heart will be selflessness, with that person as your focus, driven by a godly desire to provide for and care for his or her needs.

💬 Ask Mum & Dad

There is a wonderful chapter in the Bible (1 Corinthians 13) where we get a list of all the things that define what love *is* and what it is *not*. It explains the way that Jesus loves you, and this is a model of how you will be called to love your partner when you are married.

Read it with Mum and Dad and talk to them about how other-person-focused love is described in this chapter of the Bible.

Masturbation

The word 'masturbation' is used to describe the act of touching the genitals for pleasure.

Many boys have their first sexual feelings and ejaculate this way. Boys find their penis when they are young and soon learn that touching and stroking it feels good. At puberty sperm and semen production results in ejaculation and there are good feelings that accompany it. From what we know, fewer girls masturbate. When they do, they usually do so by touching and rubbing their genital area, especially the clitoris.

Touching the genitals in general is no different to touching another part of your body. We all touch our genitals when we bathe and wash. It is when the touching becomes a sexual act, especially when it is accompanied by sexual thoughts (called fantasies) that it becomes a problem.

We go back to brain development. Masturbating to sexual thoughts wires your growing brain to look at sexual activity as something for your personal, selfish pleasure. This will later interfere with your ability to set up a healthy sexual relationship when you are married.

Fleeting sexual feelings are normal—a sign of your brain's sexual maturation. Recognise them for what they are. Then distract yourself and move on to another activity.

Jesus is very clear about the danger of dwelling on sexual thoughts and building these into fantasies. In Matthew 5:27–28 he says that just thinking about it is as good as 'doing it'!

You are surrounded by sexual images on TV, the internet, and in movies, magazines and music videos. You may even have been exposed to porn accidentally or intentionally. Your developing sexuality will be excited by this.

⚠ Alert

Beware. Staying with the thoughts and feelings that sexual images or porn bring to your mind is unhealthy. Masturbating to them sets up dangerous wiring in your brain and sets you on a slippery slope to developing bad sexual patterns.

In 1 Peter 5:8 we read, 'Be alert and of sober mind. Your enemy the devil prowls around like a roaring lion looking for someone to devour'. Sex is a good gift from God, but Satan will try his best to tempt you to see or use sex in a bad way.

If you feel the urge to masturbate, try distracting your mind with something else you enjoy doing—the more physical the better. Or else listen to music, play a video game, or talk to a friend.

Practise self-control. The Bible is very clear about it. We need help in controlling our feelings and desires. The Apostle Paul teaches that self-control is a fruit of the Spirit (Galatians 5:22–23)—the good results of living God's way. But like fruit, self-control needs special attention so that it ripens and produces something to be enjoyed. So you just need to work on it. Above all, don't let masturbation become an easy way out when dealing with any frustrating or disappointing issues.

Finally, if you find that you have occasionally given in to the feelings and masturbated, don't feel guilty, sad or upset. Just don't allow it to become a habit.

Ask Mum & Dad

Mum and Dad were young just like you! So talk to them about any worries you have. What did their friends talk about when it came to masturbation (if anything at all)?

Maybe they can help you with some helpful ways to divert yourself when you want to masturbate.

See also | Page 42 in Part 1, **PORNOGRAPHY**

Menarche (menstrual period)

In girls, the first menstrual period is called menarche. It is a sign that your ovaries are mature and have begun producing ova (eggs), and your uterus (womb) is ready for a baby to grow in it. For a girl, this is the most dramatic sign of sexual maturity. It can happen as early as eight years or as late as 15. Along with starting your menstrual period, your body is changing. You've begun to develop breasts, pubic hair, and underarm hair. And your hips have begun to widen. Menarche also means that if you have sex, you can get pregnant. You can even get pregnant in the month before your first period starts.

From menarche you will have a menstrual period approximately once every four weeks (this can vary from month to month) until you are around 50 years old (a time called menopause).

Menarche is a normal part of growing up so accept it as just that. Don't be worried if you reach menarche early or if you are one of the last in your class.

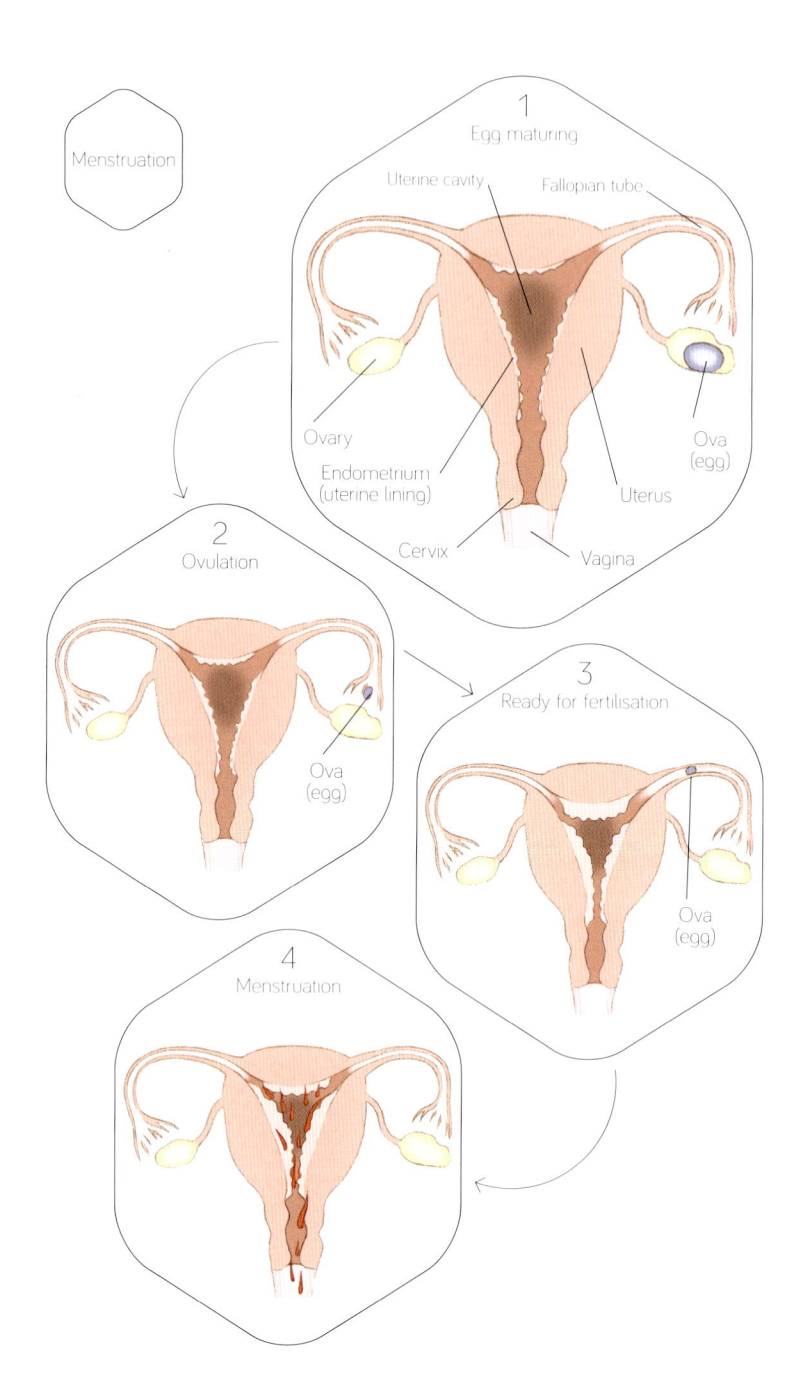

Menstruation

1 Egg maturing
- Uterine cavity
- Fallopian tube
- Ovary
- Endometrium (uterine lining)
- Cervix
- Uterus
- Vagina
- Ova (egg)

2 Ovulation
- Ova (egg)

3 Ready for fertilisation
- Ova (egg)

4 Menstruation

In some cultures, menarche is celebrated as a rite of passage from child to womanhood. Most Western cultures don't do this.

Why do girls menstruate?

Every month your uterus gets ready to accept and grow a fertilised ovum into a baby.

The ovum is released from your ovary approximately 14 days before the period begins. Think of your uterus as a nursery getting ready with all the furniture and food needed to support a baby for nine months. If you don't have sexual intercourse and/or there is no sperm to fertilise the ovum, your uterus waits 14 days and then gets rid of the 'furniture and food' stores: the inner blood-filled lining. This is why your menstrual period can sometimes feel like there are pieces of tissue with the blood.

It's called a menstrual 'cycle' because this monthly process is repeated until you are all out of ova (menopause). The first day of bleeding is taken as the first day of the cycle. The bleeding can last between two and seven days (with an average of 3–5 days) and vary in colour and thickness over this time. Some girls will find that their menstrual cycle lasts 28 days, whereas others might have a 24-day cycle, a 30-day cycle, or even longer. When you first start getting your periods, it may take a little while for your cycle to become regular and you may even miss a monthly period. Since the ovum is released about 14 days before the period happens, this is the time when a girl is most likely to get pregnant if she has sexual intercourse. The days around this are called the 'fertile period'. If you are pregnant, your period will therefore not happen. But a missed period does not automatically mean that you are having a baby; your cycle may be irregular in the first few months after menarche or changed if you do high levels of activity (if you are an athlete or ballet dancer), become ill or particularly stressed.

Ask Mum & Dad

This is probably one of the topics that you want to talk to Mum, an aunty or older sister about.

Who talked to her about menarche and menstruation?

When did she reach menarche? How did getting her periods make her feel?

What sorts of feminine products did she use during menstruation?

A tampon fits inside your vagina and is good to use when swimming or doing other physical activities. A pad has adhesive strips that help it stick to your underwear. You'll need to change tampons and pads regularly. Having a period won't prevent you from doing any of the activities you normally do. And no-one will be able to tell when you're having one.

Alert

The amount of bleeding and the timing of the menstrual period can vary from month to month in the early years of menstruation. In general the bleeding lasts from 3–5 days and the total amount of blood lost is a few tablespoons in volume (needing tampon or pad changes 4–6 times a day). It is also normal to feel some cramping pain just before or during the first day or two of bleeding.

If you are concerned about any of the following, talk to Mum and see a doctor.

> Your period lasts longer than a week.
> You have to change your pad very often (soaking more than one pad every 1-2 hours).
> You go longer than three months between periods.
> You have bleeding between periods.
> You have an unusual amount of pain before or during your period.
> Your periods were regular, but then became irregular.

Modesty

In our world of girls with plunging necklines and micro-miniskirts, and men with buff bodies and ripped abs, modesty can seem like an ancient, outdated word.

What does modesty mean? And why does it matter?

Being modest can mean not boasting about your abilities and achievements. But here we are talking modesty in terms of dressing and behaving in a way that doesn't cause sexual feelings in other people.

We need to be clear. To dress in an attractive manner is not in itself wrong. What matters is:

1 | the value you place on it. God sees into your heart. He knows your motives and the value you place on your clothes and appearance. The Apostle Paul says that, even if we feel we have a right to do what we want, not everything is good or healthy for us (1 Corinthians 6:12).

2 | the effect it has on others, particularly the opposite sex. Romans 14:12–13 reminds us: 'So then, each of us will give an account of

ourselves to God. Therefore let us stop passing judgement on one another. Instead, make up your mind not to put any stumbling block or obstacle in the way of a brother or sister'.

Think spot

What sort of dress and behaviour would be unhelpful to us and other people?

The next time you dress up for a party, look in a full-length mirror just before you walk out the door. If you met someone dressed the same way, what impressions would you have of him or her?

Why do you think some girls and boys spend so much time, money and energy on their clothes and how their bodies look?

You might want to go back and read Part 1, Chapter 4.

In the Bible, women are encouraged to dress modestly and develop an inner beauty (1 Peter 3:3–4). This is what God desires for his daughters, not because he is a killjoy but because he loves you and wants what is best for you, his child (Romans 8:15). When girls dress sexily it doesn't help their brothers in Christ. Think about what messages you are sending when you are buying clothes and getting dressed.

Boys are instructed to treat all girls as if they are their own little sister (1 Timothy 5:2). So cover up—don't intentionally expose your body, or pose in a way that draws attention to your body. Your gestures and how close you stand can make the girls around you uncomfortable.

You know that your self-worth as a Christian has nothing to do with what you wear or how you look to others. Your self-worth and identity is a given—it's as a child of God. If you place too much importance on your looks, clothes and hairstyle, it will begin to 'control' you, becoming your idol. You will begin to depend on your fashion sense and appearance to make you feel good about yourself, to feel important, or gain other people's approval.

Ask Mum & Dad

Girls: Ask Dad what sort of clothes he thinks you should wear and get him to explain why. When you are dressed for a party, ask his opinion on your clothes and make-up.

Boys: Talk to Mum (or to an aunt or other Christian woman you trust). Ask her how she thinks you should behave towards girls, both those who dress and act modestly and others who flaunt themselves. Ask Dad (or an older Christian guy you trust) what strategies he uses when he meets attractive women who don't dress modestly (remember his eyes should only be for his wife—and in the case of your father, your Mum or step-Mum!).

See also | **BODY IMAGE**

Oral sex

Oral sex is when one person places their mouth on the other person's genital area. It could be man to woman or vice versa.

Allowing someone to see your genitals—the vulva or penis—and touch or kiss them is not like holding hands with someone. When you give someone the right to see or touch your genitals, you're allowing that person to be sexually intimate with you. You're giving them entry to your most private sexual and reproductive body space. A couple at this stage of sexual intimacy would be fully or at least partially naked. Nakedness is a state where there should be mutual trust and respect—one kept for marriage where both people give each other the permission to touch, kiss and caress.

Alert

Oral sex *is* sex. Do not allow anyone to convince you that it is just a form of casual contact between two people, just for fun. It is a deeply intimate activity that should be reserved for marriage, when you can share your body in a trusting and no-shame relationship (Genesis 2:25). Also, we know that sexually transmitted infections (STIs) can be spread by oral sex.

See also | **SEXUAL INTERCOURSE**,
SEXUALLY TRANSMITTED INFECTIONS (DISEASES)

Pornography (Porn)

Pornography (or 'porn') is pictures, video or text that is created with the purpose of causing sexual excitement.

Biology textbooks and sex education material used in Health (PDHPE) class have diagrams of naked bodies and genital organs. These are not what we mean by porn. They are meant to educate boys and girls as to what their bodies look like and the changes that take place as they go through puberty. Textbooks that describe the types of behaviour that a man and a woman engage in when they are married are educational material for older teenagers and those preparing for marriage. These are not pornographic.

Online videos of sexual acts and written material that show or describe sexual acts in detail are porn—as are photographs of people engaged in sexual acts such as oral sex or intercourse. In some situations advertising billboards and magazine articles can be pornographic. Some television shows contain porn.

Let me be very clear. Pornography is not fun, innocent fantasy or a form of healthy sex education. Pornography is not about love or relationship; there is nothing tender or loving in porn images and videos. Porn is sexual material that is produced to be sold for a profit. It is harmful to anyone using it, particularly someone at your age and stage of brain development.

Where and how could you be exposed to porn?

The research tells us that many boys and girls are exposed to porn by about 11–12 years of age. We think it is happening at a much younger age for some children.

The most common way this happens is by chance. Looking online for information for a school project, for example, can take you to a site which is linked to pornographic material.

The other way it can happen is when a friend or someone in school has porn on their phone or laptop and shares it around.

What happens when a boy or girl watches porn?

Young people respond differently to porn. The response depends on the type of porn they see and how well their mum and dad have prepared them in terms of sex and their body.

There are three possible responses. All three could happen in the same person.

1 | Fear and anxiety
2 | Curiosity
3 | Sexual excitement

Why does porn have this effect?

Firstly, porn acts on the newly awakened sexual urges of your developing brain. While it is doing that, it also wires the brain circuits to accept porn sex as something that is normal and good. It basically changes the wiring in your brain. We have already discussed (pages 56–57) how everything that goes into your brain will affect the connections that are made in it.

Secondly, porn sex is a long way from God's plan for sex—it's not how he planned it to be or how he wants us to think about or use sex. But, because it is sex, it is naturally exciting.

The Bible tells us that sex is a beautiful act of intimacy (remember that 'one flesh' relationship talked about in Genesis chapters 1 and 2). It is one where a man and a woman make the commitment to care for each other and share their life together in marriage. They then trust each other completely—so completely that they can be naked and enjoy each other's bodies without feeling embarrassed or ashamed.

Porn is completely the opposite. It's about using people to portray sexual acts that are ugly and abusive. It shows people as objects to be used rather than brothers or sisters made in the image of God. The images don't show real situations that normal people experience. They are staged (set up) for the cameras and the people involved are paid to look and act in a certain way.

⚠️ Alert

What should you do if you are exposed to porn?

Here is a five-step plan which is based on the easy-to-remember term, 'Can do'.[4] Talk this over with Mum or Dad.

C: Close your eyes immediately.

Turn away and if you are on your laptop, tablet or mobile phone, turn the device off. It is quicker and easier than trying to close the webpage. Some porn is designed to open another page of pornography when you hit 'close'.

A: Alert Mum, Dad or another trusted adult (like a teacher if you are in school or a coach or supervisor if you are in a club).

Do not feel ashamed or afraid to talk to your parents or teacher about it. They are there to help you.

N: Name it

Say to yourself 'That is bad; it is pornography; I don't want anything to do with it'.

If a friend shows you porn, then tell him or her that it is unhealthy and wrong. You don't have to watch porn because your friends are doing it. Walk away if you need to.

Be an example to your friends. This may be difficult. You may even lose some friends. But they will recognise that you have chosen

---

4. This 'Can do' plan is taken from the book, *Good Pictures, Bad Pictures: Porn-Proofing Today's Young Kids*, Kristen Jenson and Gail Poyner, 2014, Glen Cove Press, California.

to live as a Christian boy or girl. And in the long term they will admire you for this. Who knows? It may even result in some of them coming to accept Jesus and become Christian.

1 Peter 2:12 says 'Live such good lives among the pagans that, though they accuse you of doing wrong, they may see your good deeds and glorify God on the day he visits us'.

D: Distract yourself.

Do something physical and fun, like riding your bike or taking a walk. Maybe you could invite a friend to play a game.

O: Order your self-control brain into action!

In Part 1 of the book we discussed how your emotional brain grows and matures faster than your control brain.

Self-control, which God gives us as a gift of the Holy Spirit (Galatians 5:22–23) is like a muscle. The more you use it, the stronger it will be. So summon it. And use it to turn away from the sexual temptation of porn.

What if you are already using porn or know a friend who is?

You need help to stop. This is not a problem you can deal with alone. Don't be embarrassed or ashamed to speak to Mum and Dad or another adult and get some help.

Ask Mum & Dad

Pornography has been around a lot longer than the internet. Ask your parents what porn was available when they were your age and how they resisted using it.

Pubic area

This is the part of your body that surrounds your genitalia: vulva and vagina in girls and penis and scrotum in boys. This area is sometimes called the crotch.

See also | **BRAZILIAN WAX AND OTHER PUBIC HAIR REMOVAL**

Self-harm

The word 'self-harm' is used to describe a practice some girls and boys use to deliberately hurt themselves. Self-harm can be a way of coping with problems. It may help you express feelings you can't put into words, distract you from your life, or release emotional pain.

All of us feel hurt and upset about things occasionally. Some of these may seem trivial or unimportant to others, including our parents. However, to the person involved, it is a big deal, and can be very upsetting. Those of you who have parents, aunties, uncles and siblings to talk to when you are upset are very blessed. Others may have youth workers and teachers they trust and can talk to.

Ask Mum & Dad

Ask them what sorts of things made them really upset and sad when they were your age.

How did they deal with these?

Sadly, some young people don't have anyone to talk to about how they are feeling. Or else, they think that no-one will understand. These are the girls and boys who sometimes use some way of harming themselves (cutting, burning or poking themselves with a sharp object) as an attempt to relieve, control or express distressing feelings. For many, self-harm is a way of asking for help, and coping with stress or emotional pain.

Sometimes it could be a symptom of a mental illness like depression and/or it may indicate that someone is considering suicide. It does not mean that they are just trying to get attention or that they are dangerous to others.

⚠ Alert

If you know anyone who is thinking of self-harm, or you notice unexplained wounds or scars, encourage them to go to their parents or a teacher. Be a friend to them and include them in your group's activities. Often young people in this situation feel like they are alone and no-one cares.

See also | **DEPRESSION**

Sexting

Sexting is the sending of sexual messages or images via mobile phone, email or another device.

Alert

At your age, sending or passing on sexy photos and explicit text messages can be classified as child pornography. This is illegal. So if you receive a photo or text with sexual content, tell your parents or your teacher immediately, and then delete it. Do not reply or forward it on to anyone else.

If anyone asks you to send them a sexy photo or starts a text conversation using sexual words, tell Mum or Dad. Don't be part of it! It might seem like harmless fun but it is serious. Other than it being against what Jesus teaches us, this behaviour could result in a criminal record for the sender and/or receiver. And having a criminal record will likely affect your ability to get a job and to travel overseas.

Sexual intercourse

Think spot

What words for having sex and sexual activity have you heard used?

Whereas 'having sex' or 'sexual activity' can be anything from holding hands and kissing to touching parts of the body and oral sex, sexual intercourse is the act of putting the man's penis into the woman's vagina. This is usually accompanied by the man's semen being deposited in the vagina (ejaculation). Other words used for sexual intercourse include coitus, 'sleeping together' and even 'going to bed'.

Sexual intercourse has been around since the dawn of time—actually, since God told the first humans to 'be fruitful and increase in number' and to 'fill the earth' (Genesis 1:28). And just like it was for the first couple, so it is for every man and woman today: once you reach puberty (girls are producing eggs, and boys, sperms) every act of sexual intercourse has the potential for a pregnancy.

For some of you the idea of two people having sexual intercourse may seem embarrassing or disgusting. That's OK—it just means that your brain and body are not ready for it yet.

Ask Mum & Dad

When and how did they learn about sexual intercourse?

How would they advise you to respond to a boy/girlfriend who says 'everyone is doing it so why can't we?'

See also | **DATING, ERECTIONS AND EJACULATIONS, SEXUALLY TRANSMITTED INFECTIONS (DISEASES)**

Sexually transmitted infections (diseases)

Sexually transmitted infections (STIs) are infections that are passed on through close body contact or the exchange of body fluids. STIs are caused by the spread of organisms like bacteria, viruses or parasites.

You can catch an infection when you have sexual intercourse. Even using a condom doesn't give you 100% protection against STIs. You can also get an STI from oral sex, anal sex and (although it's rare) by touching genitals.

See also | **ANAL SEX, ORAL SEX**

Transgender

If anyone asked you if you are a boy or a girl, you'd probably think they were trying to be funny! That's probably the only thing you're certain of right now.

Ask Mum & Dad

At what age did you realise that you were a boy or a girl?

How did you know it? Did you say something? Maybe you did (or didn't do) something?

For most of you, being a girl or a boy is something you've been certain about since you were young, even from age two.

Very rarely, something goes wrong in the developing brain, and a girl who is biologically a girl (that is has the chromosomes XX, ovaries and all the female genitalia) is convinced from an early age that she is a boy. Similarly a boy is convinced he is a girl. There are many names given to this condition—'transgender' is one of them. Other terms used are 'transsexual' and having a 'gender identity disorder' or 'gender dysphoria'.

It is important to understand that many of us go through a phase when we think it would be nice to be the other gender! Maybe a girl thinks it would be nice to be a boy because she likes to play rugby. Or a boy who enjoys cooking would rather be a girl and with Mum in the kitchen than out fishing with Dad.

Alert

These kinds of 'non-typical' interests or activities do not make a girl or boy transgendered (or homosexual, or anything else). Today we are much more accepting of boys in the kitchen and girls on the soccer field than in your parent's time. However, some boys and girls are teased and bullied for being different.

If this has happened to you, or you see others being called nasty names or bullied because they are different, tell a teacher or your parents.

See also | Page 53 in Part 1, **HOMOSEXUALITY**

Virginity

Ask Mum & Dad

What did it mean to be a virgin when you were my age?

> How important was it to stay a virgin until you were married? Was this the same for a boy as it was for a girl?

The Merriam-Webster dictionary defines a virgin as 'a person who has not had sexual intercourse' and defines sexual intercourse as 'physical sexual contact between individuals that involves the genitalia of at least one person'. So a virgin is someone who has never had any form of sexual intercourse (oral, vaginal or anal). Many teens falsely assume that they are still virgins if they have only had oral sex, but this is simply not true. Oral sex is sex, vaginal sex is sex, and anal sex is sex. Any time your sexual organs are sexually stimulated by the touch of another person, you're involved in a form of sexual activity.

Further, the term 'virginity' refers to both boys and girls.

In the Bible, the word 'virgin' is used to represent a people who are special and pure. In passages such as Isaiah 37:22 and Jeremiah 14:17, the prophets speak of Israel as a 'virgin people'. In the New Testament, the Apostle Paul wants the Church to be presented to her husband Jesus 'as a pure virgin' (2 Corinthians 11:2).

Virginity is about keeping yourself sexually pure until you are married.

You cannot lose your virginity by using a tampon or engaging in an activity such as riding a bicycle or doing gymnastics. This idea comes from the belief that the hymen (the thin membrane that lies at the entry of the vagina) is the proof of a woman's virginity, and this is stretched and sometimes torn by activity.

Think spot

How important is it to you to stay sexually pure?

Discuss this in your youth group or with friends.

What steps could you take to stay sexually pure until you are married?

See also | **ABSTINENCE, ANAL SEX, HYMEN, ORAL SEX, SEXUAL INTERCOURSE**

Wet dreams

Wet dreams are another term for when semen comes out of a boy's penis during the night. The technical word for it is nocturnal ejaculation.

The boy may be aware of it as it happens or he may not even remember. It may be associated with a dream he is having at the time.

This is just another part of a boy's sexual body waking up—another stage in the process of moving from a child to an adult. If this is happening to you, don't let it worry you. And don't be embarrassed at the wet patch on your bedsheet; Mum will understand and shouldn't make a fuss.

See also | **ERECTIONS AND EJACULATIONS**

NEXT IN THIS SERIES

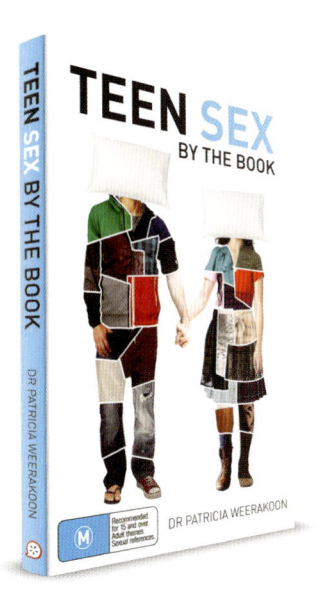

As a teenager, sex surrounds you: it's not something you need to go looking for. Perhaps you think you know it all ... or maybe that's just the impression you give your friends.

This book answers your questions about teenage sexuality and relationships. Renowned sex therapist and educator, Dr Patricia Weerakoon, explores the topics of sexual desire and arousal, falling in love, and dating—things like, 'How far is too far?' You'll also cover topics like cybersex, pornography and homosexuality, and the effects these can have on our sex lives. The discussion is frank and, in parts, explicit.

You may find it a little uncomfortable, but it's stuff that will inform and challenge you. Ultimately, it calls you to consider who you are and what you stand for. Discover how living God's counterthcultural lifestyle leads to healthy, pleasurable sex and intimate, satisfying relationships that last a lifetime.

AVAILABLE FROM

fervr.net/teen-sex-by-the-book

| HOME | TEEN LIFE | BIBLE | ENTERTAINMENT | YOUTH GROUP | VIDEOS | QUESTION |

KEEP THE CROSS CENTRAL NO MATTER WHERE YOU ARE

fervr

VISIT FERVR.NET FOR
DAILY ARTICLES, DEVOTIONS, VIDEOS AND POP CULTURE REVIEWS FOR CHRISTIAN TEENS